Teach Me
TO *Pray*

Teach Me TO *Pray*

ANDREW MURRAY

BARBOUR
PUBLISHING

INTRODUCTION

A deeper spiritual life cannot grow without deeper daily devotion to God's Word and to prayer.

No one knew this better than Andrew Murray (1828–1917). One of the best-loved and most widely read writers on the deeper Christian life, this South African pastor, preacher, and missions speaker prayed for—and witnessed—spiritual revival on three continents, and every day experienced the need for personal renewal.

If you share a hunger for God's presence, this devotional will satisfy you with an astonishing banquet. Here, thoughtfully chosen from the best of Murray's 240 books and carefully updated in today's language, are insights on prayer from Murray's writings: *Absolute Surrender, The Ministry of Intercession, The Prayer Life, The Secret of Power from On High,* and many others.

"Time alone with the Lord Jesus each day is indispensable," insisted Andrew Murray. May you begin to satisfy your hunger for God with this inspiring devotional.

Be careful for nothing;
but in every thing by prayer and supplication
with thanksgiving let your requests be made known unto God.
And the peace of God,
which passeth all understanding,
shall keep your hearts and minds through Christ Jesus.

PHILIPPIANS 4:6–7 KJV

Wait upon God

He {Daniel} *prayed* three times a day,
just as he had always done, giving thanks to his *God*.

The more I think of and pray about the religious situation in our country, the deeper my conviction becomes that Christians do not realize that the aim of conversion is to bring them into daily fellowship with the Father in heaven.

For the believer, taking time each day with God's Word and in prayer is indispensable. Each day we need to wait upon God for His presence and His love to be revealed.

It is not enough at conversion to accept forgiveness of sins or even to surrender to God. That is only a beginning. We must understand that we have no power on our own to maintain our spiritual life. We need to receive daily new grace from heaven through fellowship with the Lord Jesus. This cannot be obtained by a hasty prayer or a superficial reading of a few verses from God's Word. We must take time to come into God's presence, to feel our weakness and our need, and to wait on God through His Holy Spirit to renew our fellowship with Him. Then we may expect to be kept by the power of Christ throughout the day.

It is my aim to help Christians to see the absolute necessity of spending time with the Lord Jesus. Without this, the joy and power of God's Holy Spirit in daily life cannot be experienced.

FELLOWSHIP WITH GOD

"I have loved you even as the *Father* has loved *me*.
Remain in *my* love."

JOHN 15:9

The three Persons in the Godhead are the Father, the Son, and the Holy Spirit—each one is different from the others. God desires to reveal Himself as a person. Each one of us is an individual distinct from others and standing in certain relationships to others. God will reveal Himself to us as a person, and we are called to enter into fellowship with Him.

God greatly desires this relationship with us, but sin has come between us and our God. Even in Christians who know God, there is often great ignorance and even indifference to this personal relationship of love to God.

People believe that at conversion their sins are forgiven, that God accepts them so that they may go to heaven, and that they should try to do God's will. But they do not realize that, even as a father and his child on earth enjoy being together, so they must have this intimate fellowship with God each day.

Our relationship to Christ rests on His deep, tender love to us. We are not capable on our own to render Him this love, but the Holy Spirit will do the work in us. Meditate quietly on this thought: "'And because they love me, my Father will love them, and I will love them'" (John 14:21). Take time to experience this personal fellowship.

JESUS

You are to name *him Jesus*,
for *he* will save *his* people from their sins.

MATTHEW 1:24

The Lord Jesus was a person on this earth. He had His own individual name. His mother, His disciples, all His friends called Him by this name—Jesus. But they probably thought little of what that name meant. Nor do the majority of Christians know what a treasure is contained in that name—Jesus—"He shall save His people from their sins."

Many think about His death on the cross and His resurrection, but do they realize that He is a living person in heaven who thinks of us each day? He wants us to bring Him our love and worship.

When we first ask Jesus Christ to save us from our sins, we know very little about how this is done. The living Christ reveals Himself to us, and through the power of His love, our desire to sin is taken away. Through personal fellowship with Him, Jesus saves us from our sins. First we must come to Jesus confessing all the sin in our hearts. We must know Him as the almighty personal Savior in whom God's holiness dwells. As we fellowship together in the expression of mutual love, by the work of His Holy Spirit in our hearts, His love will expel and conquer all the sin.

ALONE WITH GOD

"When you pray, *go away by yourself,* shut *the door behind you,*
and pray *to your* Father *secretly."*

MATTHEW 6:6

Have you ever thought what a wonderful privilege it is to have the liberty of asking God to meet with you and to hear what you have to say? We should use such a privilege gladly and faithfully.

"When you pray," says Jesus, "go away by yourself, shut the door behind you, and pray to your Father secretly." This means two things. 1) Shut the world out; withdraw from all the thoughts and concerns of the day. 2) Shut yourself in alone with God to pray in secret. Let this be your chief object in prayer, to realize the presence of your heavenly Father. Let your goal be: "Alone with God."

Being alone in His presence and praying to the Father in secret is only the beginning. Come to Him in the full assurance that He knows how you long for His help and guidance. He will listen to you.

Then follows the great promise of verse 6: "Then your Father, who knows all secrets, will reward you." Your Father will see to it that your prayer is not in vain. Prayer in secret will be followed by the secret working of God in your heart.

OBEY THE WORD OF GOD

"People need more than bread for their life;
they must feed on every word of God."

MATTHEW 4:4

Bread is indispensable to life. We all understand this. However strong a person may be, if he takes no nourishment he will grow weaker and eventually die. Even so with the Word of God.

Bread must be eaten. I may know all about bread. I may give it to others. I may have bread in my house and on my table in great abundance, but that will not help me. I must eat the bread.

If through illness I am unable to eat it, I shall die. Likewise, mere knowledge of God's Word and even preaching it to others will not help me. It is not enough to think about it. I must feed on God's Word and take it into my heart and life.

Bread must be eaten daily, and the same is true of God's Word. The psalmist says: "They delight in doing everything the LORD wants; day and night they think about his law" (Psalm 1:2). "Oh, how I love your law! I think about it all day long" (Psalm 119:97). To secure a strong and powerful spiritual life, spending time in God's Word every day is indispensable. When on earth the Lord Jesus learned, loved, and obeyed the word of the Father. If you seek fellowship with Him, you will find Him in His Word.

OBEDIENCE

If you *obey me* and do whatever *I*
command you. . . .*I* will be your *God*.

JEREMIAH 44:4

God gave this command to Israel when He gave them the law, but Israel had no power to keep the law. So God gave a "new covenant" to enable His people to live a life of obedience. We read in Jeremiah 32:40: "I will make an everlasting covenant with them. . .I will put a desire in their hearts to worship me, and they will never leave me." Ezekiel 36:27 says: "I will put my Spirit in you so you will obey my laws and do whatever I command." These wonderful promises gave the assurance that obedience would be their desire.

Listen to what Jesus says about obedience in John 14:21, 23: "Those who obey my commandments are the ones who love me. And because they love me, my Father will love them, and I will love them. . . . And we will come to them and live with them."

No father can train his children unless they are obedient. No teacher can teach a child who continues to disobey him. No general can lead his soldiers to victory without prompt obedience. Ask God to imprint this lesson on your heart: The life of faith is a life of obedience. As Christ lived in obedience to the Father, so we need to live in loving obedience to God.

Do you think it's impossible for you to be obedient? It may be impossible to you, but not to God. He has promised to "put my Spirit in you so you will obey my laws." Pray and meditate on these words.

CONFESSION OF SIN

If we confess *our sins to* him, *he is faithful and just
to* forgive *us and to* cleanse *us from every wrong.*

1 JOHN 1:9

Too often the confession of sin is superficial and neglected. Few
Christians realize how absolutely necessary confession is. An
honest confession of sin gives power to live a life of victory over
sin. We need to confess with a sincere heart every sin that may
be a hindrance in our Christian lives.

Listen to what David says, "I confessed all my sins to you
and stopped trying to hide them. I said to myself, 'I will confess my rebellion to the LORD.' And you forgave me! All my
guilt is gone. For you are my hiding place; you protect me from
trouble. You surround me with songs of victory" (Psalm 32:5,
7). David speaks of a time when he was unwilling to confess his
sin. "When I refused to confess my sin, I was weak and miser-
able" (verse 3). But when he had confessed his sin, a wonderful
change came.

Confession means not only that I confess my sin with shame
and repentance, but that I turn it over to God, trusting Him to
take it away. Such confession implies that I am unable to get rid
of my guilt unless, by an act of faith, I trust God to deliver me.
This deliverance means that I know my sins are forgiven and
that Christ undertakes to cleanse me from the sin and keep me
from its power.

THE FIRST LOVE

"But I have this complaint against you. You don't love me or each other as you did at first!"

REVELATION 2:4

In Revelation 2:2–3, eight signs are mentioned showing the zeal of the church at Ephesus, but there was one bad sign. The Lord said: "Turn back to me again and work as you did at first. If you don't, I will come and remove your lampstand from its place among the churches" (verse 5). What was this sin? "You don't love me or each other as you did at first!" (verse 4).

We find the same sin in the church today. There is enthusiasm for the truth, there is continuous hard work, but what the Lord values most is missing: tender, fervent love for Him.

A Christian may be a good example in all he does, yet the tender love for Jesus is missing. There is no personal, daily fellowship with Christ. All the many activities with which people satisfy themselves are nothing in the eyes of the Master.

Dear friend, this book speaks of the fellowship of love with Christ and spending time in His presence. Everything depends on this. Christ came from heaven to love us just as the Father loved Him. He suffered to win our hearts for this love. His love can be satisfied with nothing less than deep personal love.

Christ considers this of prime importance. Let us do so, too. Even though we are doing many good things "for the Lord," we must not leave "our first love."

THE HOLY SPIRIT

*"He will bring me glory by revealing
to you whatever he receives from me."*

JOHN 16:14

The last night that He was with His disciples, Jesus promised to send the Holy Spirit as a Comforter. Although His bodily presence was removed, they would realize His presence in them and with them in a wonderful way. The Holy Spirit of God would reveal Christ in their hearts so that they would experience His presence with them continually. The Spirit would glorify Christ and would reveal to them the glorified Christ in love and power.

Do not fail to understand, to believe, and to experience this wonderful truth. Doing the Lord's work is not a duty performed in one's own strength. No, that is impossible; it is the Holy Spirit alone who will teach us to love Him sincerely.

God must have entire possession of us. He claims our whole heart and life. He will give us the strength to have fellowship with Christ, to keep His commandments, and to abide in His love. Once we have grasped this truth, we will begin to feel our deep dependence on the Holy Spirit and ask the Father to send Him in power into our hearts.

CHRIST'S LOVE TO US

"I have loved you even as the Father has loved me.
Remain in my love."

JOHN 15:9

In relationships between friends and relatives, everything depends on their love to each other. What value is wealth if love is lacking between husband and wife, or parents and children? What value is knowledge and enthusiasm in God's work without the knowledge and experience of Christ's love? (See 1 Corinthians 13:1–3.) Christians need to know by experience how much Christ loves them, and to learn how they may abide and continue in that love.

Christ says: "As the Father has loved Me"—that is a divine, everlasting, wonderful love! "I also have loved you." The same love with which He had loved the Father He now gives us. He really desires that this everlasting love should rest upon us. What a blessing! Christ wants us to live in the power of the love of God that He also experienced.

In your fellowship with Christ in private or in public, you are surrounded by God's love. Jesus longs to fill you with His love.

Read from time to time what God's Word says about the love of Christ. Meditate on the words and let them sink into your heart. Sooner or later you will begin to realize: The greatest happiness of your life is that you are loved by the Lord Jesus and can live in fellowship with Him every day.

OUR LOVE TO CHRIST

You *love him* even though you have never *seen him.*
Though you do not *see him,* you *trust him.*

1 PETER 1:8

People who had never seen Christ still truly loved Him and believed on Him. Their hearts were filled with unspeakable joy. Such is the life of a Christian who really loves the Lord.

The chief attribute of the Father and of the Son is love to each other and love to man. This should be the chief characteristic of the true Christian. Life becomes a well of living water, flowing out as love to the Lord Jesus.

This love is not merely a happy feeling. It is an active principle. It takes pleasure in doing the will of the Lord. It is joy to keep His commandments. As the love of Christ was shown to us by His death on the cross, our love must be exhibited in unselfish, self-sacrificing lives. Please understand this: In the Christian life, love to Christ is everything!

Great love results in great faith—faith in His love to us, faith in the powerful revelation of His love in our hearts, faith that He will work all His good pleasure in us. The wings of faith and love will lift us up to heaven and we shall be filled with joy beyond words. The joy of the Christian is an indispensable witness to the world of the power of Christ to change hearts and to fill them with love and gladness.

Take time daily in His presence to drink in His love.

LOVE TO CHRISTIANS

"So now I am giving you a new commandment:
Love each other."

Jesus told His disciples that as the Father had loved Him, even so He loved them. And now, following His example, we must love one another with the same love. "Your love for one another will prove to the world that you are my disciples" (John 13:35). He had prayed: "My prayer for all of them is that they will be one, just as you and I are one, Father—that just as you are in me and I am in you, so they will be in us, and the world will believe you sent me" (John 17:21). If we exhibit the love that was in God toward Christ, and in Christ to us, the world will be obliged to confess that our Christianity is genuine.

This is what actually happened. The Greeks and Romans, Jews and heathen, hated each other. Between all the nations of the world there was hardly a thought of love. The very idea of self-sacrifice was a strange one. When unbelievers saw that Christians from different nations, under the powerful working of the Holy Spirit, loved one another even to the point of self-sacrifice in times of need—they were amazed. They said: "Behold, how these people love one another!"

Often Christ's love is not evident among Christians. Ask God to enable you to love your fellow believers as Christ loves you.

Teach Me to *Pray*—19

PERSEVERING PRAYER

Keep on *praying*.

One of the greatest drawbacks to the life of prayer is that the answer does not come as quickly as we expect. We are discouraged and think: "Perhaps I do not pray right." So we do not persevere. Jesus often talked about this. There may be a reason for the delay and the waiting may bring a blessing. Our desire must grow deeper and stronger, and we must ask with our whole heart. God puts us into the practicing school of persevering prayer so that our weak faith may be strengthened.

Above all God wants to draw us into closer fellowship with Him. When our prayers are not answered we learn that the fellowship and love of God are more to us than the answers of our requests, and then we continue in prayer.

Do not be impatient or discouraged if the answer does not come. "Always be prayerful." "Keep on praying." You will find real blessing in doing so. Ask whether your prayer is really in accordance with the will of God and the Word of God. Ask if it is in the right spirit and in the name of Christ. You will learn that the delay in the answer is one of the most precious ways God gives you His grace.

Those who have persevered before God are those who have had the greatest power in prayer.

INTERCESSION

Pray at all times and on every
occasion in the power of the Holy Spirit.

EPHESIANS 6:18

Will God really make the pouring out of blessing on others dependent on our prayers? Yes, He makes us His fellow workers. He has taken us into partnership in His work. If we fail to do our part, others will suffer and His work will suffer.

God has appointed intercession as one of the means by which others will be saved and Christians built up in the faith. People all over the world will receive life and blessing through our prayers. Should we not expect God's children to endeavor with all our strength to pray for God's blessing on the world?

Begin to use intercession as a means of grace for yourself and for others. Pray for your neighbors. Pray for sinners that they may come to Christ. Pray for your minister and for missionaries. Pray for your country and for government leaders. If you live a life completely for God, you will realize that the time spent in prayer is an offering pleasing to God.

Yes, "pray at all times. . .and be persistent in your prayers for all believers everywhere." In so doing you will learn the lesson that intercession is the chief means of bringing others to Christ and bringing glory to God.

Prayer and Fasting

Jesus told them. . ."But this kind of demon
won't leave unless you have *prayed* and *fasted*."

MATTHEW 17:21

Jesus teaches us that a life of faith requires both prayer and fasting. Prayer grasps the power of heaven, fasting loosens the hold on earthly pleasure.

Jesus Himself fasted to get strength to resist the devil. He taught His disciples that fasting should be in secret, and the Father would reward it openly. Abstinence from food, or moderation in taking it, helps to focus on communication with God.

Let's remember that abstinence, moderation, and self-denial are a help to the spiritual life. After having eaten a hearty meal, one does not feel much desire to pray. To willingly sacrifice our own pleasure or enjoyment will help to focus our minds more fully on God and His priorities. The very practice needed in overcoming our own desires will give us strength to take hold of God in prayer.

Our lack of discipline in prayer comes from our fleshly desire of comfort and ease. "Those who belong to Christ Jesus have nailed the passions and desires of their sinful nature to his cross and crucified them there" (Galatians 5:24). Prayer is not easy work. For the real practice of prayer—taking hold of God and having communion and fellowship with Him—it is necessary that our selfish desires be sacrificed.

Isn't it worth the trouble to deny ourselves daily in order to meet the holy God and receive His blessings?

THE WORLD

When you *love* the world, you do not
have the love of the Father in you.

1 JOHN 2:15

John teaches us what he means by the world in 1 John 2:16. He says: "For the world offers only the lust for physical pleasure, the lust for everything we see, and pride in our possessions. These are not from the Father. They are from this evil world."

Because all mankind has fallen through sin, we have come under the power of the world and are deceived by the god of this world. The world with its pleasures surrounds the Christian each day with temptations.

This was the case with Eve in the Garden of Eden. We find in Genesis the three characteristics John mentions: 1) The lust of the flesh—"The woman saw that the tree was good for food." 2) The lust of the eyes—"It was pleasant to the eyes." 3) The pride of life—"A tree to be desired to make one wise" (Genesis 3:6 KJV). Our life in the world is full of danger—so much to occupy our eyes and our hearts, so much worldly wisdom and knowledge.

So John tells us: "Stop loving this evil world and all that it offers you, for when you love the world, you show that you do not have the love of the Father in you." Just as the Lord called His disciples, He calls us to leave all and follow Him.

THE STRENGTH OF THE CHRISTIAN

A final word: Be strong with
the Lord's mighty power.

EPHESIANS 6:10

Since we as Christians have no strength of our own, where may we get it? Notice the answer: Be strong with the Lord's mighty power.

Paul had spoken of this power in the earlier part of Ephesians (1:17–20). He had prayed to God to give them the Spirit that they might know the greatness of His power which He displayed when He raised Christ from the dead. This is the literal truth: the greatness of His power which raised Christ from the dead works in every believer. We hardly believe it and much less experience it. That is why Paul prays that God would teach us to believe in His almighty power.

In Ephesians 3:16–17, Paul asks the Father to strengthen them by His Spirit, that Christ might dwell in their hearts. And then in verse 20: "Now glory be to God! By his mighty power at work within us, he is able to accomplish infinitely more than we would ever dare to ask or hope."

Read over these scriptures again and pray for God's Spirit to make these words real to you. Believe in the divine power working in you. Pray that the Holy Spirit may reveal it to you. Appropriate the promise that God will show His power in your heart, supplying all your needs. It is clear that much time is needed with the Father and the Son, if you would experience the power of God within you.

CHRIST IN ME

Examine yourselves to see if
your faith is really genuine.

2 CORINTHIANS 13:5

Christ is in me. What a difference it would make if we could take time every morning to focus on the thought: Christ is in me.

Christ made it clear to His disciples. The Spirit would teach them: "When I am raised to life again, you will know that I am in my Father, and you are in me, and I am in you" (John 14:20). Through the power of God, we who believe were crucified with Christ and raised again with Him. As a result Christ is in us! Through faith in God's Word, the Christian accepts it.

Paul expresses this thought in the prayer of Ephesians 3:16: "I pray that from his glorious, unlimited resources he will give you mighty inner strength through his Holy Spirit." Notice that it is not the ordinary gift of grace, but a special revelation of the riches of His love that Christ may dwell in your heart by faith. Have you been able to grasp that?

Paul said: "I fall to my knees and pray to the Father" (Ephesians 3:14). That is the only way to obtain the blessing. Take time in prayer in His presence to realize: "Christ dwells in me." Even in the midst of your daily schedule, look upon your heart as the dwelling place of the Son of God. Then Christ's words: "Those who remain in me, and I in them, will produce much fruit" (John 15:5) will become your daily experience.

THE LOVE OF THE SPIRIT

He has given us the *Holy Spirit*
to fill our hearts with *his* love.

ROMANS 5:5

As God's children, we must confess that we know very little of fervent, childlike love for our heavenly Father. Why is this? Perhaps we have not learned the lesson that there must be a constant renewal of faith in what God is able to do. We try to stir up love toward God in our hearts. Yet, in our own strength, we cannot awaken the slightest love to God.

Child of God, believe that the love of God will work as the power in your heart that enables you to love God and to love others. Cease to expect love in yourself. Believe in the power of God's love resting on you and teaching you to love God with His own love.

Learn the lesson of our text: "He has given us the Holy Spirit to fill our hearts with his love." The Spirit will enable us to love God, our friends, and even our enemies. Be assured of two things. First, in your own strength you cannot love God or your fellow Christians. And second, the Holy Spirit is within you every day and every hour, seeking to fill you with the Spirit of love. Each morning as you commit yourself into the keeping of the Holy Spirit, let this prayer arise:

Lord, grant me the assurance that You will pour forth the love of Christ into my own heart, and then let it stream forth to all around me! Amen.

As God Forgives

"And *forgive* us our sins—just as we
forgive those who have sinned against us."

LUKE 11:4

The forgiveness of sins is the one great gift that sets the sinner free. Forgiveness gives us boldness toward God and is the source of our salvation. The forgiveness of sins gives us a reason to be thankful every day of our lives.

As we walk with God in the assurance of sins forgiven, He desires that we should live as those who have been freely forgiven. We can only prove our sincerity by forgiving those who have offended us as willingly as God has forgiven us.

In the Lord's Prayer we are taught to pray: "Forgive us our sins—just as we forgive those who have sinned against us." Then at the end: "But if you refuse to forgive others, your Father will not forgive your sins" (Matthew 6:15). In Matthew 18:21 we have the question of Peter: "Lord, how often should I forgive someone who sins against me?" Our Lord answered, "Seventy times seven!"

Then follows the parable of the servant whose lord forgave him his debt but who would not show compassion on his fellow servant. His lord asked: "Shouldn't you have mercy on your fellow servant, just as I had mercy on you?" So the servant was sent to prison. The Lord warns us: "That's what my heavenly Father will do to you if you refuse to forgive your brothers and sisters in your heart" (Matthew 18:33, 35).

LOVE AND PRAYER

Be earnest and disciplined in your prayers.
Most important of all, *continue* to
show deep love for each other.

4 PETER 4:7–8

Earnest prayer and fervent love are closely linked. If we pray only for ourselves, we will not find it easy to be in the right attitude toward God. But when our hearts are filled with love for others, we will continue to pray for them, even for those with whom we do not agree.

Prayer holds an important place in the life of love; they are inseparably connected. If you want your love to increase, forget yourself and pray for God's children. If you want to increase in prayerfulness, spend time loving those around you, helping to bear their burdens.

There is a great need for earnest, powerful intercessors! God desires His children to present themselves each day before the throne of grace to pray down the power of the Spirit upon all believers. Unity is strength. Spiritual unity will help us to live unselfishly, wholly for God and others. Let us apply Peter's words to our lives—"earnest in prayer. . .showing deep love for each other."

As we meditate on love to those around us, we will be drawn into fellowship with God. This will come, not by reading or thinking, but by spending time with the Father and with the Lord Jesus through the Holy Spirit. Love leads to prayer—to believing prayer is given the love of God.

A Song of Love

There are three things that will *endure*—faith, hope, and love—
and the greatest of these is love.

1 Corinthians 13:13

Today is wholly devoted to the praise of love. The first three
verses of 1 Corinthians 13 speak of the absolute necessity of love
as the chief thing in our religion. "If I could speak in any language in heaven or on earth. . .if I had the gift of prophecy. . .
if I had the gift of faith so that I could speak to a mountain
and make it move. . .if I gave everything I have to the poor and
even sacrificed my body. . .but if I didn't love others" then, three
times repeated, "I would only be making meaningless noise like
a loud gong or a clanging cymbal. . .what good would I be? . . .
I would be of no value whatsoever." If I have not love, I am of no
value.

There are fifteen things said about love, but one sentence
sums up its whole nature: "It does not demand its own way"
(verse 5). And again: "Love will last forever" (verse 8). Prophecies,
unknown languages, and knowledge shall vanish away. Even faith
and hope shall be changed into sight. But love lasts forever.

"Love does not demand its own way." Think and pray about
this. "Love will last forever." Consider all that means. "The
greatest of these is love." Let this love rule in your life.

God is love. "God is love, and all who live in love live in
God, and God lives in them" (1 John 4:16). Let your heart be
filled with love so that, by God's almighty power, you may be a
witness to the transforming power of love. Then you will be a
blessing to all around you.

THE LOVE THAT SUFFERS

Live a life filled with love for others, following
the example of *Christ*, who *loved* you and *gave*
himself as a sacrifice to take away your sins.

EPHESIANS 5:2

It is strange that love, which is the source of the greatest happiness, should also be the cause of the most intense suffering. Suffering always follows when love seeks to save the object of its love. It is only by suffering that love can gain its end and so attain the highest happiness.

Even the almighty power of God's love could not achieve its purpose without suffering. By suffering, Christ bore the sins of the whole world. Love in the midst of suffering manifested the greatest glory and attained its end perfectly.

Love worthy of the name manifests itself in a life of continual self-sacrifice. Love gives strength to endure, whatever the circumstances. Loving others may mean tears, heartache, and much persevering in prayer; but love overcomes all obstacles.

Do you long to know the love of Christ in all its fullness? Then yield yourself to Him. Think of yourself as a channel through which the highest love can reach its aim. Begin to suffer with and intercede for those around you. Eventually you will realize what this life of love is: to live wholly for the welfare and happiness of others.

TIME FOR PRAYER

Yet no one *calls* on *your* name
or *pleads* with *you* for mercy.

ISAIAH 64:7

At a ministerial meeting the superintendent of a large district said: "I rise in the morning and have half an hour with God. I am occupied all day with numerous engagements. Not many minutes elapse without my breathing a prayer for guidance. After work I speak to God of the day's work. But I know little of the intense prayer of which scripture speaks."

There are earnest Christians who have just enough prayer to maintain their spiritual position but not enough to grow spiritually. Seeking to fight off temptation is a defensive attitude rather than an assertive one which reaches for higher attainment. The scriptural teaching to cry out day and night in prayer must, to some degree, become our experience if we are to be intercessors.

A man said to me, "I see the importance of much prayer, and yet my life hardly allows time for it. Am I to give up? How can I accomplish what I desire?"

I admitted that the difficulty was universal and quoted a Dutch proverb: "What is heaviest must weigh heaviest." The most important must have the first place. The law of God is unchangeable. In our communication with heaven, we only get as we give. Unless we are willing to pay the price—to sacrifice time and attention and seemingly necessary tasks for the sake of the heavenly gifts—we cannot expect much power from heaven in our work.

STONE WALLS GIVE WAY

But while Peter was in prison,
the church *prayed* very earnestly for him.

ACTS 12:5

When we pray consistently we will receive an entrance into God's will of which we would otherwise know nothing. We will receive blessing above all we ask or think. The teaching and power of the Holy Spirit are unalterably linked to prayer.

The power that the Church's prayer has is shown not only as the apostles pray but also as the Christian community does. In Acts 12 Peter is in prison awaiting execution. The death of James had aroused the Church to a sense of great danger; the thought of losing Peter, too, wakened all their energies. They went to prayer.

Prayer was effective; Peter was delivered. When he came to the house of Mary he found "many were gathered for prayer" (Acts 12:12). Double chains, soldiers, and the iron gate—all gave way before the power from heaven that prayer brought to his rescue. The power of the Roman Empire was nothing in the presence of the power that the Church wielded in prayer.

Those Christians stood in close and living relationship with their Lord. They knew well that the words "I have been given complete authority" and "Be sure of this: I am with you always" were absolutely true. They had faith in His promise to hear them whatever they asked. They prayed in the assurance that the powers of heaven not only could work on earth but also that they would work at the Church's request on its behalf.

A MODEL OF INTERCESSION

They will *pray* to the L̃O̅R̃D̃ day and night
for the fulfillment of *his* promises.
Take no rest, all you who pray.

ISAIAH 62:6

"Then, teaching them more about prayer, he [Jesus] used this illustration: 'Suppose you went to a friend's house at midnight, wanting to borrow three loaves of bread. You would say to him, "A friend of mine has just arrived for a visit, and I have nothing for him to eat." He would call out from his bedroom, "Don't bother me. The door is locked for the night, and we are all in bed. I can't help you this time." But I tell you this—though he won't do it as a friend, if you keep knocking long enough, he will get up and give you what you want so his reputation won't be damaged'" (Luke 11:5–8).

Prayer is the one power on earth that commands the power of heaven. The early days of the Church are a great object lesson of what prayer can do. Prayer can pull down the treasures of heaven into earth.

Prayer is both indispensable and irresistible. Unknown blessing is stored up for us in heaven; that power will make us a blessing to men and enable us to do any work or face any danger. It is the one secret of success. It can defy all the power of the world and prepare men to conquer that world for Christ.

In all this prayer there was little thought of personal need or happiness. Rather there was desire to witness for Christ and bring Him and His salvation to others. It was the thought of God's kingdom and glory that possessed these disciples. We, too, must enlarge our hearts for the work in intercession.

WILLING LOVE

*"A friend of mine has just arrived for a visit,
and I have nothing for him to eat."*

LUKE 11:6

The friend took his weary, hungry friend into his house and into his heart, too. He did not excuse himself by saying he had no bread. At midnight he went out to seek food for him. He sacrificed his night's rest and his comfort to find the needed bread. "Love does not demand its own way" (1 Corinthians 13:5). It is the very nature of love to forget itself for the sake of others. It takes their needs and makes them its own. It finds real joy in living and dying for others as Christ did.

The love of a mother for her prodigal son makes her pray for him. When we have true love for others we will have the spirit of intercession.

It is possible to do much faithful and earnest work for others without true love for them. Just as a lawyer or a physician, out of a love of their profession and a high sense of faithfulness to duty, may become deeply involved with the needs of clients or patients without any special love for them, so servants of Christ may give themselves to their work with devotion and self-sacrificing enthusiasm without any strong, Christlike love.

It is this lack of love that causes a lack of prayer. Love will compel us to prayer as that love and diligence are combined with the tender compassion of Christ.

THE SENSE OF INADEQUACY

*"Don't bother me. The door is locked for the night,
and we are all in bed. I can't* help *you this time."*

LUKE 11:7

We often speak of the power of love. In one sense this is true, and yet the truth has limitations. The strongest love may be utterly inadequate. A mother might be willing to give her life for her dying child but still not be able to save it. The host at midnight was most willing to give his friend bread, but he had none. It was this sense of inadequacy that sent him begging, "A friend of mine has just arrived. . .and I have nothing for him to eat." This sense of inadequacy gives strength to the life of intercession.

"I have nothing for him to eat." As we are aware of our inadequacies, intercession becomes the only hope and refuge. I may have knowledge, a loving heart, and be ready to give myself for those under my charge, but I cannot give them the bread of heaven. With all my love and zeal, still "I have nothing to set before them."

Blessed are you if you have made "I have nothing" the motto of your ministry. You think of the judgment day and the danger of those without Christ and recognize a supernatural power is needed to save people from sin. You feel utterly insufficient—all you can do is to meet their natural need. "I have nothing" motivates you to pray. Intercession appears to you as the only thing in which your love can take refuge.

Persistency That Prevails

*"Don't bother me. The door is locked for the night,
and we are all in bed. I can't help you this time."*

LUKE 11:7

The faith of the host in Luke 11 met a sudden and unexpected obstacle—the rich friend refuses to hear: "I can't help you this time." The loving heart had not counted on this disappointment and cannot accept it. The asker presses his threefold plea: Here is my needy friend; you have abundance; I am your friend. Then he refuses to accept a denial. The love that opened his house at midnight and then left it to seek help must conquer.

Here is the central lesson of the parable: in our intercession we may find that there is difficulty and delay in the answer. It may be as if God says, "I can't help you this time." It is not easy to hold fast our confidence that He will hear and then to continue to persevere in full assurance that we shall have what we ask. Even so, this is what God desires from us.

He highly prizes our confidence in Him, which is essentially the highest honor the creature can render the Creator. He will therefore do anything to train us in the exercise of this trust in Him. Blessed the man who is not staggered by God's delay or silence or apparent refusal, but is strong in faith giving glory to God. Such faith perseveres, importunately if need be, and cannot fail to inherit the blessing.

STRENGTHENING PRAYER LIFE

"Listen to me! You can *pray* for anything,
and if you *believe*, you will have it."

MARK 11:24

The consequence of sin that makes it impossible for God to give at once is a barrier on God's side as well as ours. The attempt to break through the power of sin is what makes the striving and the conflict of prayer such a reality.

Throughout history people have prayed with a sense that there were difficulties in the heavenly world to overcome. They pleaded with God for the removal of the unknown obstacles. In that persevering supplication they were brought into a state of brokenness, of entire resignation to Him, and of faith. Then the hindrances in themselves and in heaven were both overcome. As God prevails over us, we prevail with God.

God has made us so that the more clearly we see the reasonableness of a demand, the more heartily we will surrender to it. One cause of our neglecting prayer is that there appears to be something arbitrary in the call to such continued prayer. This apparent difficulty is a divine necessity and is the source of unspeakable blessing.

Try to understand how the call to perseverance and the difficulty that it throws in our way is one of our greatest privileges. In the very difficulty and delay will the true blessedness of the heavenly life be found. There we learn how little we delight in fellowship with God and how little we have of living faith in Him. There we learn to trust Him fully and without reservation. There we truly come to know Him.

PERSISTENCE IN PRAYER

"You can pray for anything,
and if you believe, you will have it."

MARK 11:24

Persistence has various elements—the main ones are perseverance, determination, and intensity. It begins with the refusal to readily accept denial. This develops into a determination to persevere, to spare no time or trouble, until an answer comes. This grows in intensity until the whole being is given to God in supplication. Boldness comes to lay hold of God's strength. At one time it is quiet; at another, bold. At one point it waits in patience, but at another, it claims at once what it desires. In whatever different shape, persistence always means and knows that God hears prayer; I must be heard.

Think of Abraham as he pleads for Sodom. Time after time he renews his prayer until he has to say, "Please don't be angry, my Lord" (Genesis 18:30). He does not cease until he has learned how far he can go, has entered into God's mind, and has rested in God's will. For his sake Lot was saved. "God had listened to Abraham's request and kept Lot safe" (Genesis 19:29).

Think of Jacob when he feared to meet Esau. The angel of the Lord met him and wrestled with him. When the angel saw that he did not prevail, he said, "Let me go." Jacob said, "I will not let you go" (Genesis 32:26). So the angel blessed him there. That boldness pleased God so much that a new name was given to Jacob: Israel, he who strives with God, "because you have struggled with both God and men and have won" (Genesis 32:28).

THE MARK OF A
PRAYING CHRISTIAN

The earnest prayer of a righteous person
has great power and wonderful results.

JAMES 5:16

Remember the marks of the true intercessor: a sense of the need of those without Christ, a Christlike love, an awareness of personal inadequacy, faith in the power of prayer, courage to persevere in spite of refusal, and the assurance of an abundant reward. These are the qualities that change a Christian into an intercessor.

These are the elements that mark the Christian life with beauty and health. They fit a person for being a blessing in the world. These are the attitudes that call forth the heroic virtues of the life of faith.

Nothing shows more nobility of character than the spirit of enterprise and daring which battles major difficulties and conquers. So should we who are Christians be able to face the difficulties that we meet in prayer. As we "work" and "strive" in prayer, the renewed will asserts its royal right to claim what it will in the name of Christ.

We should fight our way through to the place where we can find liberty for the captive and salvation for the perishing. The blessings which the world needs must be called down from heaven in persevering, believing prayer.

Our work is often insignificant due to our little prayer. Let us change our method and make unceasing prayer be the proof that we look to God for everything and that we believe that He hears us.

The Life That Can Pray

*"I chose you. I appointed you to go and produce
fruit that will last, so that the Father will give
you whatever you ask for, using my name."*

John 15:16

Our power in prayer depends upon our life. When our life is right, we will know how to pray in a way pleasing to God, and our prayer will be answered. "If you stay joined to me," our Lord says, "you may ask any request you like, and it will be granted" (John 15:7). According to James it is the prayer of a righteous man that "has great power and wonderful results" (James 5:16).

In the parable of the vine Jesus taught that the healthy, vigorous Christian may ask what he or she wishes and will receive it. He says, "If you stay joined to me and my words remain in you, you may ask any request you like, and it will be granted." Again He says, "You didn't choose me. I chose you. I appointed you to go and produce fruit that will last, so that the Father will give you whatever you ask for, using my name" (John 15:16).

What life must one lead to bear fruit? What must a person be in order to pray with results? What must one do to receive what he or she asks? The answer is simple. Live as a branch depending on the vine for strength. The source of power in prayer is the vine. If we are branches, abiding in Christ, the vine, He will supply the power. If we trust the vine, then we can ask what we wish and it will be granted.

BEARING FRUIT

The earnest prayer of a righteous person
has great power and wonderful results.

JAMES 5:16

A branch is a growth of the vine, produced to bear fruit. It has only one purpose: that through it the vine may bear and ripen its fruit. As the vine lives to produce the sap that makes the grape, so the branch receives that sap and bears the grape. Its work is to serve the vine so that, through the branch, the vine may do its work.

The believer, the branch of Christ the heavenly Vine, is to live exclusively so Christ may bear fruit through him. A true Christian is to be devoted to the work of bearing fruit to the glory of God.

With our life abiding in Him, and His words abiding and ruling in our heart, there will be grace to pray as we should and faith to receive whatever we ask.

The promises of our Lord's farewell discourse appear to us too large to be taken literally. We rationalize them to meet our human ideas of what we think they ought to be. We separate them from the life of devotion to Christ's service for which they were given.

God's covenant is: give all and take all. One who is willing to be nothing but a branch of Christ, the Vine, will receive liberty to claim Christ's riches in all their fullness and the wisdom and humility to use them properly.

PRUNING FOR PRAYER

"He prunes the branches that do bear fruit
so they will produce even more."

JOHN 15:2

The more aware we become of our inability to pray in power, the more we are helped to press on toward the secret of power in prayer. Jesus said, "I am the true vine, and my Father is the gardener" (John 15:1). We not only have Jesus Himself. We have the Father, as the husbandman, watching over our growth and fruit-bearing. It is not left to our faith. God Himself will see to it that the branch is what it should be. He will enable us to bring forth just the fruit we were appointed to bear. "He prunes the branches that do bear fruit so they will produce even more." The Father seeks more fruit. More fruit is what the Father Himself will provide.

Of all fruit-bearing plants there is none that produces so much wild wood as the vine. Every year it must be pruned. It is like this for the Christian. The branch that desires to abide in Christ and bring forth fruit must yield itself to divine cleansing.

The gardener cuts away true, honest wood that the branch has produced. It must be pruned because it draws away the strength of the vine and hinders the flow of the juice to the grape. The luxuriant growth of wood must be cast away so that abundant life may be seen in the cluster.

There are things in you that sap away your interest and strength. They must be pruned. Pruning results in a life that can pray.

Is Prayerlessness Sin?

*"I will not remain with you any longer
unless you destroy the things among you
that were set apart for destruction."*

JOSHUA 7:12

If we are to deal effectively with the lack of prayer, we must ask, "Is it sin?" Jesus is Savior from sin. When we experience sin, we can know the power that saves from sin. The life that can pray effectively is one that knows deliverance from the power of sin. But is prayerlessness sin?

Experiencing the presence of God is the great privilege of God's people and their power against the enemy. Throughout scripture the central promise is that God is with us. The whole-hearted person lives consciously in God's presence.

Defeat and failure are due to the loss of God's presence. This was true at Ai. God brought His people into Canaan with the promise of victory. With the defeat at Ai, Joshua knew that the cause must be the withdrawal of God's power. God had not fought for them.

In the Christian life defeat is a sign of the loss of God's presence. If we apply this to our failure in prayer, we see that it is because we are not in full fellowship with God.

The loss of God's presence is due to sin. Just as pain is nature's warning of a physical problem, defeat is God's voice telling us there is something wrong. He has given Himself wholly to His people. He delights in being with them. He never withdraws Himself unless they compel Him to do so by sin.

REVEALED SIN

"As for me, I will certainly not *sin* against the
Lord by ending my prayers for you. And I will
continue to teach you what is good and right."

1 Samuel 12:23

We may think we know what sin is keeping us from prayer, but only God can truly reveal it. For example, after the defeat at Ai, He spoke to Joshua. "Israel has sinned and broken my covenant" (Joshua 7:11). Israel had sinned. God Himself revealed it.

God must reveal to us that the lack of prayer is a greater sin than we have thought. It means we have little taste for fellowship with God. Our faith rests more on our own work than on the power of God. We are not ready to sacrifice ease for time with God.

When the pressure of work becomes the excuse for not finding time in His presence, there is no sense of absolute dependence upon God. There is no full surrender to Christ.

If we would yield to God's Spirit, all our excuses would fall away and we would admit that we had sinned. Samuel once said, "As for me, I will certainly not sin against the Lord by ending my prayers for you. And I will continue to teach you what is good and right" (1 Samuel 12:23). Ceasing from prayer is sin against God.

When God discloses sin it must be confessed and cast out. If we have reason to think prayerlessness is the sin that is in "our camp," let us begin with personal and united confession. With God's help let us put away and destroy the sin. Then we can know His presence and power.

GOD'S PRESENCE RESTORED

Restore to me again the
joy of *your* salvation.

PSALM 51:12

When sin is cast out, God's presence is restored. This truth is so simple. God's presence restored means victory secured. Then, if there is defeat, we are responsible for it. Sin somewhere is causing it. We need to discover the sin and repent. The moment the sin is put away, we may confidently expect God's presence.

God never speaks to His people of sin except with the purpose of saving them from it. The same light that shows the sin will show the way out of it. The same power that condemns will give the power to rise up and conquer.

God is speaking to us about this sin: "He was amazed to see that no one intervened to help the oppressed" (Isaiah 59:16). The God who says this will work the change in His children when they seek His face. He will make the shame of sin confessed a door of hope. Let us simply confess that we have sinned; we dare not sin any longer.

In the matter of prayer God does not demand impossibilities. He does not give us an impracticable ideal. He does not ask us to pray without giving the grace to enable us to do so. Believe Him. He will give the grace to do what He asks.

DESIRE

"You can *pray* for anything,
and if you *believe*, you will have it."

MARK 11:24

Desire is the power that moves our whole world and directs the course of each person. Desire is the soul of prayer. The cause of insufficient prayer is often the lack of desire. Some may doubt this. They are sure they have earnestly desired what they ask. But if they judge whether their desire has been as wholehearted as God would have it, they may see that it was the lack of desire that caused the failure.

What is true of God is true of each of His blessings. "If you look for me in earnest, you will find me when you seek me" (Jeremiah 29:13).

We may have a strong desire for spiritual blessings. But alongside them are other desires occupying a large place in our interests. The spiritual desires are not all-absorbing. We are puzzled that our prayer is not heard. It is because God wants the whole heart. If there are desires which occupy more of our heart than He Himself, the desires that we are praying for cannot be granted.

We desire the gift of intercession, grace and power to pray as we should. Our hearts must give up other desires; we must give ourselves wholly to this one. By focusing on the blessedness of this grace, by believing with certainty that God will give it to us, desire may be strengthened. The first step will have been taken toward the possession of the desired blessing.

EXPRESS YOUR DESIRES

"You can *pray* for anything,
and if you *believe*, you will have it."

MARK 11:24

The desire of the heart must become the expression of the lips. The Lord Jesus more than once asked those who cried out to Him what they wanted. He wanted them to say what they desired. To declare it brought them into contact with Him and wakened their expectation. To pray is to enter into God's presence, to have distinct dealing with Him, to commit our need to Him, and to leave it there. In so doing we become fully conscious of what we are seeking.

There are some who often carry strong desires in their heart but don't bring them to God in a clear expression of repeated prayer. There are others who go to the Word and its promises to strengthen their faith but do not pointedly ask God to fulfill them. Therefore their heart does not gain the assurance that the matter has been put into God's hands. Still others come in prayer with so many requests and desires that it is difficult for them to say what they really expect God to do.

If you want God to give you this gift of faithfulness in prayer and power to pray as you should, begin to pray about it. Declare to yourself and to God.

FAITH

"You can pray for anything,
and if you believe, you will have it."

MARK 11:24

It is only by faith that we receive Jesus Christ or live the Christian life. Faith also is the power of prayer. If we are to have our prayer for the grace of prayer answered, we must begin to pray in faith as never before.

Faith is the opposite of sight. They are contrary to each other. "We live by believing and not by seeing" (2 Corinthians 5:7). If heart and prayer are to be full of faith, we must withdraw from the visible. The person that seeks to enjoy life, who gives first place to the duties of daily life, is inconsistent with a strong faith.

"We don't look at the troubles we can see right now." The negative action needs to be emphasized if the positive "rather, we look forward to what we have not yet seen" (2 Corinthians 4:18) is to become natural to us. In praying, faith depends upon our living in the invisible world.

The reason for our lack of faith is our lack of knowledge of God and communion with Him. Jesus said to have faith in God when He spoke of removing mountains. When a soul knows God and allows the light of God to illuminate his life, unbelief will become impossible. All the mysteries connected with answers to prayer—however little we may be able to solve them intellectually—will be swallowed up in the assurance that this God is our God. He does answer prayer. He will delight to give the grace to pray that I am asking for.

ACCEPT THE ANSWER

"You can pray for anything,
and if you believe, you will have it."

MARK 11:24

Faith must accept the answer given by God in heaven before it is found on earth. This is the essence of believing prayer. Spiritual things can only be spiritually grasped. The spiritual blessing of God's answer to your prayer must be accepted in your spirit before you see it physically. Faith does this.

A person who not only seeks an answer, but first seeks after the God who gives the answer, receives the power to know that he has obtained what he has asked. If he knows that he has asked according to God's will, he believes that he has received.

There is nothing so heart-searching as this faith, "if you believe, you will have it." As we strive to believe, and find we cannot, we are compelled to discover what hinders us. Blessed are those who, with their eyes on God alone, refuse to rest till they have believed what our Lord bids. Here is the place where faith prevails, and prevailing prayer is born out of human weakness. Here enters the real need for persevering prayer that will not rest or go away or give up till it knows it is heard and believes that it has received.

EXPERIENCE THE BLESSING

*"You can pray for anything,
and if you believe, you will have it."*

MARK 11:24

Receiving from God in faith the answer with perfect assurance that it has been given, is not necessarily the possession of the gift we have asked for. At times there may be a long interval before we have it physically. In other cases we may enjoy at once what we have received. When the interval is long we have need of faith and patience. We need faith to rejoice in the assurance of the answer bestowed and to begin to act upon that answer though for the present there is no visible proof of its presence.

We can apply this principle to our prayer for the power to be faithful intercessors. Hold fast to the divine assurance that as surely as we believe, we receive. Rejoice in the certainty of an answered prayer. The more we praise God for it, the sooner will the experience come. We may begin at once to pray for others in the confidence that grace will be given us to pray with more perseverance and more faith than we have done before.

If we do not find an immediate increase in our desire to pray, this must not discourage us. We have accepted a spiritual gift by faith; in that faith we are to pray, doubting nothing. We may count upon the Holy Spirit to pray in us, even though it is with groanings which cannot find expression. In due time we shall become conscious of His presence and power.

THE OMNIPRESENCE OF CHRIST

"I will be with you."

EXODUS 3:12

When Christ said to His disciples, "I have been given complete authority in heaven and on earth," the promise immediately followed, "I am with you always" (Matthew 28:18, 20). The Omnipotent One is truly the Omnipresent One. The writer of Psalm 139 speaks of God's omnipresence as something beyond his comprehension: "Such knowledge is too wonderful for me, too great for me to know!" (verse 6).

The revelation of God's omnipresence in the man Christ Jesus makes the mystery still deeper. The fact that we can experience this presence every moment is inexpressibly wonderful. And yet many of us find it difficult to understand all that Christ's presence implies and how, through prayer, it can become the practical experience of our daily life.

When Christ says "always," He means to give us the assurance that there should never be a moment in which that presence cannot be our experience. Yet, it does not depend upon what we can effect, but upon what He undertakes to do.

The omnipotent Christ is indeed the omnipresent Christ. His promise to us is: "I am with you always." Let your faith in Christ, the Omnipresent One, be in the quiet confidence that He will be with you every day and every moment. Meet Him in prayer, and let His presence be your strength for service.

MARY: THE MORNING WATCH

"Mary!" *Jesus* said. She *turned* toward
him and *exclaimed*, "Teacher!"

JOHN 20:16

Here we have the first manifestation of the risen Savior—to Mary Magdalene, the woman who loved Jesus so much.

Think of what the morning watch meant to Mary. Is it not a proof of the intense longing of a love that would not rest until it had found the Lord? It meant a separation from all else in her longing to find Christ. It meant the struggle of fear against a faith that refused to let go its hold of Christ's wonderful promise: "Those who obey my commandments are the ones who love me. . .and I will love them. And I will reveal myself to each one of them" (John 14:21).

That first morning watch, waiting in prayer for the risen Lord to reveal Himself, has been a joy to thousands of souls! With a burning love and strong hope, they wait for Jesus to manifest Himself as the Lord of Glory. There they learn to dwell in the keeping of His abiding presence.

There is nothing that can prove a greater attraction to our Lord than the love that sacrifices everything and rests satisfied with nothing less than Himself. It is to such a love that Christ reveals Himself. He loved us and gave Himself for us. It is to our love that He speaks the word: "And be sure of this: I am with you always" (Matthew 28:20). It is love that accepts, rejoices, and lives in that word.

EMMAUS: THE EVENING PRAYER

As they *sat* down to eat. . . . Suddenly,
their eyes were opened, and they *recognized him*.

LUKE 24:30-31

Mary teaches us what the morning watch can mean for the revelation of Jesus to the soul. Emmaus reminds us of the place that the evening prayer has in preparing for the full manifestation of Christ in the soul.

When Jesus Himself approached the two disciples as they traveled, they did not recognize Him. But as the Lord spoke with them, their hearts began to burn within them. Yet they never thought that it might be Christ Himself. How often does Jesus come near with the purpose of manifesting Himself to us, and yet we don't see Him?

When Jesus told the two disciples He must continue on His journey, their plea to spend the night caused Him to stay. We, too, should reserve time toward the end of the day when our whole heart prays with the urgency that constrains Him.

So what was it that led our Lord to reveal Himself to these two men? Nothing less than this: their intense devotion to their Lord. There may be much ignorance and unbelief, but if there is a burning desire that longs for Christ, He will make Himself known to us. In such intense devotion and constraining prayer, the Lord will open our eyes and we will know Him and enjoy the secret of His abiding presence.

Why Could We Not?

"But this kind of demon won't leave
unless you have prayed *and* fasted."*

The disciples had often cast out demons. But here they had been powerless. They asked the Lord what the reason might be. His answer is very simple: "You didn't have enough faith."

How is it that we cannot live that life of unbroken fellowship with Christ which the scripture promises? Simply because of our unbelief. We do not realize that faith must accept and expect that God will, by His almighty power, fulfill every promise He has made. We do not live in that utter helplessness and dependence on God alone which is the very essence of faith. We are not strong in the faith, fully persuaded that what God has promised He is able and willing to perform.

But what is the reason why this faith is so often lacking? "But this kind of demon won't leave unless you have prayed and fasted." To have a strong faith in God requires a life in close touch with Him by persistent prayer. We cannot call up faith at our bidding; it needs close communion with God through prayer. It needs the denial of self—the sacrifice of a worldly heart. Just as we need God to give us faith and power, He, too, needs our whole being to be utterly given up to Him. Prayer and fasting are essential to this.

THE POWER OF OBEDIENCE

"And the one who sent me is with me—
he has not deserted me. For I always do
those things that are pleasing to him."

JOHN 8:29

In these words Christ tells us what His life with the Father was. At the same time He reveals the law of all communion with God—simple obedience.

In John 14 He says three times: "If you love me, obey my commandments" (vs. 15, 21, 23); also in chapter 15: "When you obey me, you remain in my love, just as I obey my Father and remain in his love. You are my friends if you obey me" (vs. 10, 14).

Obedience is the proof and the exercise of the love of God in our hearts. It comes from love and leads to love. It assures us that we are abiding in the love of Christ. It seals our claim to be called the friends of Christ. So it is not only a proof of love but of faith, too. It assures us that we "will receive whatever we request because we obey him and do the things that please him" (1 John 3:22).

Obedience enables us to abide in His love and gives us the full experience of His unbroken presence. It is to the obedient that the word comes: "And be sure of this: I am with you always" (Matthew 28:20) and to whom all the fullness of its meaning will be revealed.

THE POWER OF FAITH

"Anything is possible
if a person believes."

MARK 9:23

Scripture teaches us that there is not one truth on which Christ insisted more frequently than the absolute necessity of faith and its unlimited possibilities.

Experience has taught us that there is nothing in which we fall so short as the simple and absolute trust in God to literally fulfill in us all He has promised. A life in Christ's abiding presence must of necessity be a life of unceasing faith.

What are the marks of true faith? First of all, faith counts upon God to do all He has promised. It seeks nothing less than to claim every promise that God has made, in its largest and fullest meaning. It trusts the power of an almighty God to work wonders in the heart in which He dwells and rests in the hope of what He will do.

In the pursuit of the power which such a life of faith can give, our soul must take God at His word and claim the fulfillment of His promises. We must then look to Him, even in utter darkness, to perform what He has spoken.

The life of faith to which the abiding presence will be granted must have complete mastery of our whole being. This faith will be able to claim and experience the words of the Master: "And be sure of this: I am with you always" (Matthew 28:20).

PAUL'S MISSIONARY MESSAGE

For this is the secret: *Christ lives* in you, and this is your
assurance that you will share in *his* glory.

COLOSSIANS 1:27

In Paul's mind, the very substance of his Gospel was the indwelling Christ. He spoke of the "riches of the glory of this mystery—Christ in you, the assurance of glory." Though he had preached this Gospel for so many years as a missionary, he still asked for prayer that he might make that secret known.

The complaint is often made in regard to our churches that, after a time, there appears to be no further growth and very little of the joy and power for bearing witness to Christ Jesus. The question comes whether the church at home is living in the experience of this indwelling Christ, so that the sons and daughters whom she sends out also know the secret. The answer is in Paul's missionary message which culminates in the words: "Christ. . .in you. . .your assurance that you will share in his glory."

Paul deeply felt the need for prayer to enable him to give this message faithfully. Is there not a call to all those who pray for our missionaries, and to our missionaries themselves, to obtain the power that leads Christians into the enjoyment of their rightful heritage? May the church at home also share in the blessing of this truth.

THE HOLY SPIRIT

*"He {the Holy Spirit} will bring me glory by revealing
to you whatever he receives from me."*

JOHN 16:14

When our Lord spoke the words to the disciples in Matthew
28:20 "And be sure of this: I am with you always," they did not
at first understand or experience their full meaning. At Pentecost they were filled with the Holy Spirit. It was then that the
Spirit brought down into their hearts the new life of Christ's
abiding presence.

All our attempts to claim to live that life of continuous
communion with Christ will be in vain unless we yield ourselves completely to the power and indwelling of the Holy
Spirit. For the Spirit of God to show us what He can enable
us to be, He demands complete possession of our whole being.

Christ meant the promise of His abiding presence to be
accepted as absolute, divine truth. "And God has given us his
Spirit as proof that we live in him and he in us" (1 John 4:13).
But this truth can only be experienced when the Spirit of God
is known and believed in and obeyed.

We need to understand that the Holy Spirit came as God to
make known the Son in us. He claims absolute subjection and
is willing to take possession of our whole being and will enable
us to fulfill all that Christ asks of us.

THE CHRIST LIFE

Christ lives in me.

GALATIANS 2:20

Christ's life was more than His teaching, more than His work, even more than His death. It was His life in the sight of God and man that gave value to what He said and did and suffered. It is this life that He gives to His people and enables them to live it out before men.

It was the life in the new brotherhood of the Holy Spirit that made both Jews and Greeks feel that there was some superhuman power about Christ's disciples. They gave living proof of the truth that God's love had come down and taken possession of them.

Everything depends upon the life with God in Christ being right. It is the simplicity and intensity of our life in Christ Jesus, and of His life in us, that sustains us in our daily walk. It makes us conquerors over self and everything that could hinder the Christ life. Through prayer, it gives us the victory over the powers of evil.

The life in Christ must be everything to us because Christ Himself lives in us. When Jesus spoke the words "And be sure of this: I am with you always" (Matthew 28:20), He meant nothing less than this: "All day and every day, I am with you. I am the secret of your life, your joy, and your strength."

Exceeding Abundantly

By *his* mighty power at work within us,
he is able to accomplish infinitely more
than we would ever dare to ask or hope.

EPHESIANS 3:20

In the great prayer which Paul had just written, he had apparently reached the highest expression possible of the life to which God's mighty power could bring the believer. But Paul is not content. In this doxology he rises still higher and lifts us up to give glory to God as "able to accomplish infinitely more than we would ever dare to ask or hope." Pause for a moment to consider what "infinitely more" means.

Think of the words, "he has given us all of his rich and wonderful promises" (2 Peter 1:4). Think of "the incredible greatness of his power for us who believe him. This is the same mighty power that raised Christ from the dead" (Ephesians 1:19–20). With these words Paul hopes to lift our hearts to believe that God is able to do "infinitely more than we would ever dare to ask or hope." The power of God that works in us is nothing less than the exceeding power that raised Christ from the dead. This should cause us to think that there is something that God will do in us that is beyond all our imagination.

As we worship Him in prayer, let us believe that the Almighty God, who is working in our hearts, is able and willing to fulfill every one of His exceeding great and precious promises.

THE FRUIT OF THE SPIRIT

But when the Holy Spirit controls our lives, he will produce this kind of fruit in us: love, joy, peace. . . .

GALATIANS 5:22

The first two lessons on prayer are: We must ask the Father to give us the Spirit anew every morning, and then ask the Spirit to teach us and help us. Here is a third lesson—commit to memory today's text.

Christians often think that they only need to ask God to teach them to pray and that He will do it at once. This is not always the case. What the Spirit does is strengthen our spiritual lives so we are able to pray better. When we ask Him to teach us, it is important that we first of all surrender ourselves to the working of the Spirit. This surrender consists in naming before Him the fruit of the Spirit, with the earnest prayer to be filled with this fruit.

Think of the first three—love, joy, peace—the three chief characteristics of a strong faith life. Love: to God, to believers, and to all men. Joy: the proof of the provision for every need of courage and faith for all the work we have to do. Peace: the blessed state of undisturbed rest and security in which God can keep our hearts and minds.

In His last talk with the disciples, Christ used these words: "remain in his love. . .so that you will be filled with my joy" (John 15:10–11). "I am leaving you with a gift—peace of mind and heart" (John 14:27).

INTERCESSION

Pray for each other.

JAMES 5:16

There is value in intercession. It is an indispensable part of prayer. It strengthens our love and faith in what God can do, and it brings blessing and salvation to others. Prayer should be mainly for others, not for ourselves alone. Begin by praying for those near and dear to us, those with whom we live, that we may be of help to them and not a hindrance.

Pray for your friends and all with whom you come into contact. Pray for all Christians, especially for ministers and those in responsible positions.

Pray for those who do not yet know the Lord as their Savior. Make a list of the names of those God has laid upon your heart and pray for their conversion. Christ needs you to bring to Him in prayer the souls of those around you. Pray, too, for all poor and neglected ones. Pray for mission work. Use a mission calendar with daily subjects of prayer.

Do you think this will take too much time? Just think what an inconceivable blessing it is to help others through your prayers. Look to the Holy Spirit for further guidance. If morning is not the best time for you, schedule another time later in the day. Cultivate the attitude: "I am saved to serve."

TIME

"Couldn't you stay awake and
watch with *me* even one hour?"

MATTHEW 26:40

Every minute spent in prayer is valuable. If ten minutes is all the time you can give, see what you can do in that time. Most people can spare more time. If you will only persevere from day to day, time will come of its own accord.

Is it possible that Christians can say that they cannot afford to spend a quarter or half an hour alone with God and His Word? When a friend comes to see us or we have to attend an important meeting or there is anything to our advantage or pleasure, we find time easily enough.

But God has a right to us and longs for us to spend time with Him, and we find no time for fellowship with Him. Even God's own servants are so occupied with their own work that they find little time for that which is all-important—waiting on God to receive power from on high.

Dear child of God, let us never say "I have no time for God." Let the Holy Spirit teach us that the most important and profitable time of the whole day is the time we spend alone with God. Communion with God through His Word and prayer is as indispensable to us as the food we eat and the air we breathe. Whatever else is left undone, God has the first and foremost right to our time.

THE WORD OF GOD

For the word of *God* is
full of living power.

HEBREWS 4:12

I find it a great help to use God's Word in my prayers. If the Holy Spirit impresses a certain text upon my mind, I plead the promise. This habit increases our faith, reminds us of God's promises, and brings us into harmony with God's will. We learn to pray according to God's will and understand that we can only expect an answer when our prayers are in accordance with that will (1 John 5:14).

Prayer is like fire. Fire can only burn brightly if it is supplied with good fuel. That fuel is God's Word which must be studied carefully and prayerfully. His Word must be taken into the heart and lived out in the life.

We are all familiar with the characteristics of a seed—a small grain in which the life-power of a whole tree slumbers. If it is placed in the soil, it will grow and increase and become a large tree. Each word or promise of God is a seed containing a divine life in it. If I carry it in my heart by faith, love it, and meditate on it, it will slowly, surely spring up and bring forth the fruit of righteousness.

The Holy Spirit uses both the Word and prayer. Prayer is the expression of our human need and desire. The Holy Spirit teaches us to use the Word as a guide to what God will do for us.

THE SPIRIT GLORIFIES CHRIST

"He will bring me glory by revealing
to you whatever he receives from me."

JOHN 16:14

To understand and experience the work of the Holy Spirit you must try to grasp the relationship of the Holy Spirit to the Lord Jesus. Our Lord said that the Spirit would come as a Comforter to the disciples. The Spirit would reveal Him in their hearts. The disciples held on to that promise—they would not miss their Lord but have Him with them always. This made them pray earnestly for the Holy Spirit, for they longed to have Jesus with them always.

This is the meaning of our text—"He will bring me glory by revealing to you whatever he receives from me." Where there is an earnest desire for the glory of Jesus in the heart of the believer, the Holy Spirit will preserve the presence of Jesus in our hearts. We must not weary ourselves with striving after God's presence. We must quietly endeavor to abide in fellowship with Christ, to love Him and keep His commandments, and to do everything in the name of Jesus. Then we will be able to count upon the secret but powerful working of the Spirit within us.

If our thoughts are always occupied with the Lord Jesus—His love, His joy, His peace—then the Holy Spirit will graciously bring the fruit of the Spirit to ripeness within us.

THE FELLOWSHIP OF THE SPIRIT

The fellowship of the
Holy Spirit be with you all.

2 CORINTHIANS 13:13–14

In this verse we have one of the main characteristics and activities of the Holy Spirit. It is through the Holy Spirit that the Father and Son are one and have fellowship with each other.

We also have fellowship with the Father and the Son through the Spirit. "Our fellowship is with the Father and with his Son, Jesus Christ" (1 John 1:3). "And we know he lives in us because the Holy Spirit lives in us" (1 John 3:24). Through the Spirit we know the fellowship of love with the Father and Son.

Through the Spirit we, as God's children, have fellowship with each other. With the child of God there should be no selfishness. We are members of one Body. Through the Spirit the unity of the Body must be maintained. One reason that the Spirit does not work with greater power in the church is that the unity of the Spirit is not sought after. At Pentecost, after ten days spent in united prayer, the one hundred and twenty seemed melted together into one body. They received the Spirit in fellowship with each other.

We have fellowship when we meet at the communion table; we also have fellowship one with another in the trials of other members of the Body. Our text reminds us: "The fellowship of the Holy Spirit be with you all."

In heaven there is an eternal fellowship of love between Father and Son through the Spirit. Do we really long to be filled with the Spirit?

WITH THE WHOLE HEART

*"If you look for me in earnest,
you will find me when you seek me."*

JEREMIAH 29:13

It's often been said that if one seeks to perform any great work, he must do it with his whole heart and with all his might. In business this is the secret of success. Above all in spiritual things it is indispensable, especially in praying for the Holy Spirit.

Let me repeat that the Holy Spirit desires to have full possession of you. He can be satisfied with nothing less if He is to show His full power in your life.

Do you realize when you pray for the Holy Spirit that you are praying for the whole Godhead to take possession of you? Have your prayers had a wrong motive? If you were expecting that God would do something in your heart but in other things you would be free to do your own will, that would be a great mistake. The Holy Spirit must have full possession.

You may not feel a burning, urgent desire for the Holy Spirit to have full control, and you do not see any chance of its becoming true in your life. God knows about this inability of yours; He has ordained that the Holy Spirit will work within you all you need. What God demands of us, He will work within us. On our part there must be earnest prayer each day and an acceptance of the Holy Spirit as our leader.

Child of God, the Holy Spirit longs to possess you wholly. Submit yourself in complete dependence on His promise.

WALK IN THE SPIRIT

Live according to your new life in the Holy Spirit. . . .
If we are living now by the Holy Spirit, let us *follow* the Holy
Spirit's leading in every part of our lives.

GALATIANS 5:16, 25

The Christian in his daily walk must follow the leading of the Spirit. That will be the sign of a spiritual person who serves God in the Spirit and does not trust in his own abilities.

The Spirit is not needed just when we pray or just for our work for God's kingdom. God gives us His Spirit to be in us the whole day. We need Him most in the middle of our daily work because there the world has such power to lead us away from God. We need to ask the Father every morning for a fresh renewal of His Spirit. During the course of the day, let us remind ourselves that the Spirit is with us.

Paul says: "Now, just as you accepted Christ Jesus as your Lord, you must continue to live in obedience to him" (Colossians 2:6). Again: "Put ye on the Lord Jesus Christ" (Romans 13:14 KJV). Just as we put on a coat when we go out, so we must put on the Lord Jesus. We must show by our conduct that Christ lives in us and that we walk by the Spirit.

"Live according to your new life in the Holy Spirit. Then you won't be doing what your sinful nature craves" (Galatians 5:16). If we are not under the guidance of the Holy Spirit, we will do things in our own strength. The Spirit is given to teach us that we may walk by the Spirit at all times.

THE SPIRIT PROMISED
TO THE OBEDIENT

*"If you love me, obey my commandments.
And I will ask the Father, and he will give you
another Counselor, who will never leave you."*

JOHN 14:15–16

Christ would ascend to heaven and ask the Father to send the Comforter, the Holy Spirit. He would not do this only once, but it would become part of His intercessory work. He would "live forever to plead with God on their behalf" (Hebrews 7:25).

The Lord tells us in John 14 on what conditions He will send the Spirit: if we love Him and keep His commandments, "I will ask the Father." The Holy Spirit is given to enable us to do the will of the Father. The conditions are reasonable and just. As we keep the commandments through the Spirit, the Spirit will be granted to us in fuller measure. Let us say to God that we will strive to keep His commands.

Do not listen to the whispers of Satan or give way to unbelief. Surrender yourself unreservedly to the Lord who has said: "If you love me, obey my commandments." Love will enable you to do it. Trust the Lord Jesus with childlike faith and give yourself completely to do His will—that is all that is necessary. Then the beauty of the divine agreement that He makes with us will become reality: "When you obey me, you remain in my love" (John 15:10). The Father will send the Holy Spirit anew each day.

Rivers of Living Water

"If you believe in *me, come* and *drink*!
For the scriptures *declare* that rivers of
living water will flow out from within."

John 7:38

Jesus, in His conversation with the Samaritan woman, said: "The water I give them takes away thirst altogether. It becomes a perpetual spring within them, giving them eternal life" (John 4:14). In John 7:38 the promise is even greater: rivers of living waters flowing from him, bringing life and blessing to others. John says that this refers to the Holy Spirit who would come when Christ had been glorified.

What do we need in order to experience the rivers of living water? Just one thing: the inner connection to Christ—the unreserved surrender to fellowship with Him. We have the firm assurance that His Spirit will work in us what we cannot do. We need a faith that rejoices in the divine power and love. We need a faith that depends on Him day by day to grant us grace that living water may flow out from us.

If the water from a reservoir is to flow into a house all day, one thing is necessary: The connection must be perfect. Then the water passes through the pipe of its own accord. So the connection between us and Christ must be uninterrupted. Our faith must accept Christ and depend on Him to sustain the new life.

ALL THE DAY—EVERY DAY

I will bless you every day.

PSALM 145:2

It is a step forward in the Christian life when you seek to have fellowship with God in His Word each day without fail. Perseverance will be crowned with success if you are really sincere. The experience may be somewhat as follows:

When you wake up in the morning, God will be your first thought. Set apart a time for prayer and resolve to give God time to hear requests and to reveal Himself. You may share all your desires with God and expect an answer.

Later on in the day, even if only for a few minutes, take time to keep up the fellowship with God. And again in the evening take time to reflect on the day's work and, with confession of sin, receive the assurance of forgiveness. Then commit yourself anew to God and His service.

Gradually you will get an insight into what is lacking in life and will be ready for uninterrupted fellowship with God through the Holy Spirit. You will gain the assurance through faith that the Holy Spirit, the Lord Jesus, and the Father Himself will give His presence and help all through the day.

Remember that you only need to live life one day at a time. You don't have to worry about tomorrow but rest in the assurance that He who has led you today will be even closer tomorrow.

THE SPIRIT AND PRAYER

"The truth is, you can go directly to the
Father and *ask him*, and *he* will grant
your request because you *use my* name."

JOHN 16:23

In Jesus' farewell discourse (John 13–17), He presented life in the Spirit in all its power and attractiveness. Through the Holy Spirit God's children can go directly to the Father and ask God to bless the world. Seven times we have the promise repeated: "You can ask for anything in my name, and I will do it" (John 14:13–14; 15:7, 16; 16:23–24, 26). Read these passages over so that you may come to understand how urgently and earnestly our Lord repeated the promise.

During the ten days before Pentecost the disciples proved this. In response to their continuous united prayer, the heavens were opened. The Spirit of God descended to earth, filling them with His life. They received the power of the Spirit that they might impart it to thousands. That power is still the pledge of what God will do. If God's children will agree with one accord to wait for the promise of the Father each day, there is no limit to what God will do for them.

Christian, remember that the Holy Spirit will dwell in you with divine power, enabling you to testify for Him. But it also means that you may unite with God's children to ask in prayer greater and more wonderful things than the heart can imagine.

BECOMING EDUCATED

*I urge you. . .to pray for all people. As you make
your requests, plead for God's mercy upon them,
and give thanks. Pray this way for. . .all. . .
who are in authority.*

1 TIMOTHY 2:4–2

Pray without ceasing. How can we learn to do that? The best
way of learning to do a thing—in fact the only way—is to do
it. Begin by setting apart some time every day, say ten or fifteen
minutes, in which you say to God and to yourself that you
come to Him now as intercessor for others. It can be in the
morning, in the evening, or any other time. Do not worry if
you cannot set aside the same time every day. Just see that you
do it. Christ chose you and appointed you to pray for others.

If at first you do not feel any special urgency, faith, or power
in your prayers, do not let that hinder you. Quietly tell the
Lord Jesus of your weakness. Believe that the Holy Spirit is in
you to teach you to pray. Be assured that, if you begin, God will
help you. God cannot help you unless you begin and keep on.

Pray at all times. How do I know what to pray for? Once
you begin to think of all the needs around you, you will soon
find enough to pray for. But to help you, each day for the next
few weeks we will concentrate on subjects and hints for prayer.
Use and reuse these ideas until you know more fully to follow
the Spirit's leading and have learned, if need be, to make your
own list of subjects. These days can be a time of becoming edu-
cated in this matter of praying at all times.

WHAT TO PRAY

Pray for each other.

JAMES 5:16

Scripture calls us to pray for many things: for all Christians, for all men and women, for all in government, and for all who are in adversity. It tells us to pray for sending missionaries, for those in the ministry of the Gospel, for believers who have fallen into sin, for those in our own circle of friends. The Church is now much larger than when the New Testament was written. The number of ministries and workers is much greater. The needs of the Church and the world are so much better known that we must take time to see where prayer is needed and to what our heart is most drawn.

The scriptural calls to prayer demand a large heart, taking in all saints, and all men and women, and all needs. An attempt will be made these next days to indicate what the chief subjects are that need prayer and that ought to interest every Christian.

It may be difficult to pray for such large spheres as are sometimes mentioned. Where one subject appears of more special interest or more urgent than another, spend some time day after day to pray about that. If you really give time to intercession and the spirit of believing intercession is cultivated, the object is accomplished. While the heart must be enlarged at times to take in all, the more pointed and definite our prayer can be, the better.

GOD IS SUFFICIENT

My gracious favor is all you need.

2 CORINTHIANS 12:9

Who is sufficient for real intercession? The more we study and try to practice the grace of intercession, the more we feel overwhelmed by its greatness and our weakness. Let that feeling lead you to hear: "My gracious favor is all you need," and to answer truthfully, "Our only power and success come from God" (2 Corinthians 3:5).

Take courage; you are called to take part in the intercession of Christ. The burden and the agony, the triumph and the victory, are all His. Learn from Him; to know how to pray, yield to His Spirit in you. He gave Himself as a sacrifice to God for us that He might have the right and power of intercession. "He bore the sins of many and interceded for sinners" (Isaiah 53:12).

Let your faith rest boldly on His finished work. Let your heart identify with Him in His death and His life. Like Him, give yourself to God as a sacrifice for others. It is your highest calling, your true and full union with Him.

Come and give your whole heart and life to intercession, and you will know its blessedness and its power. God asks nothing less; the world needs nothing less; Christ asks nothing less; let nothing less be what we offer to God.

THE POWER OF THE HOLY SPIRIT

*I pray that. . .he will give you mighty
inner strength through his Holy Spirit.*

EPHESIANS 3:16

Pray for the full manifestation of the grace and energy of the Holy Spirit to remove all that is contrary to God's revealed will. Do this so that we do not grieve the Holy Spirit. Then He can work with mightier power in the Church for the exaltation of Christ and for our blessing.

All prayer unites in the one request—the power of the Holy Spirit. Make it your prayer.

Pray as a child asks a father. "You fathers—if your children ask for bread, do you give them a stone? . . . If you sinful people know how to give good gifts to your children, how much more will your heavenly Father give the Holy Spirit to those who ask him" (Luke 11:11, 13).

Ask as simply and trustfully as a child asks for food. You can do this because "God has sent the Spirit of his Son into your hearts, and now you can call God your dear Father" (Galatians 4:6). This Spirit is in you to give you childlike confidence. Have faith in the fact that He is praying in you. In that faith ask for the power of the Holy Spirit everywhere. Mention places or groups where you especially desire it to be seen.

THE SPIRIT OF HOLINESS

"Make them pure and holy by
teaching them *your* words of truth."

JOHN 17:17

God is the Holy One. His people are a holy people. He speaks: "I, the LORD, am holy, and I make you holy" (Leviticus 21:8). Christ prayed: "Make them pure and holy by teaching them your words of truth" (John 17:17). Paul prayed: "Christ will make your hearts strong, blameless, and holy when you stand before God" (1 Thessalonians 3:13). "May the God of peace make you holy in every way" (1 Thessalonians 5:23).

Pray for all the believers—God's holy ones—throughout the Church. Pray that the Spirit of holiness may rule them. Especially pray for new converts. Pray for the believers in your own neighborhood or congregation, especially for any you are interested in. Think of their special need, weakness, or sin, and pray that God may make them holy.

Pray, trusting in God's omnipotence. The things that are impossible with men are possible with God. Often when we ask for great things, we think there is little likelihood of their happening. Prayer is not only wishing or asking, but believing and accepting. Be still before God and ask Him to allow you to know Him as the Almighty One and leave your requests with Him who does wonders.

KEPT FROM THE WORLD

"Holy Father, keep them and care for them. . .
I'm not asking you to take them out of the world,
but to keep them safe from the evil one."

JOHN 17:11, 15

Pray that God's people may be kept from the world. The night before He was crucified, Christ asked three things for His disciples: 1) that they might be kept and cared for as those who are not of the world; 2) that they might be purified; 3) that they might be one in love. You cannot do better than to pray just as Jesus prayed. Ask that God's people may be kept separate from the world and the evil one. Pray that they, by the Holy Spirit, may live as those who are not of the world.

Pray with confidence before God. "Dear friends, if our conscience is clear, we can come to God with bold confidence. And we will receive whatever we request because we obey him and do the things that please him" (1 John 3:21–22).

Memorize that verse. Get the words into your heart. Join the ranks of those who, like John, draw near to God with an assured heart that does not condemn them. Learn to have confidence toward God. In the quiet confidence of an obedient child, pray for those believers who sin (1 John 5:16). Pray for all to be kept from the evil one. And say often, "What we ask, we receive, because we keep and do."

THE SPIRIT OF LOVE
IN THE CHURCH

When the *Holy Spirit* controls our lives,
he will produce this kind of fruit in us: love.

GALATIANS 5:22

"That they may be one, as we are—I in them and you in me. . . . Then the world will know that you sent me and will understand that you love them as much as you love me. . .that your love for me may be in them and I in them" (John 17:22–23, 26). Believers are one in Christ, as He is one with the Father. The love of God rests on them and can dwell in them. Pray that the power of the Holy Spirit will put this love in believers so that the world may see and know God's love in them. Pray consistently for this.

Pray as one of God's reminders: "I have posted watchmen on your walls; they will pray to the LORD day and night for the fulfillment of his promises. Take no rest, all you who pray" (Isaiah 62:6).

Study these words until your whole soul is filled with the realization: I am appointed as an intercessor. Enter God's presence with that faith. Approach the world's need with this thought: It is my job to intercede. Meditate on the fact that the Holy Spirit will teach you how to pray and what to pray for. Let it be a constant awareness: My great life work, like Christ's, is intercession. My purpose is to pray for believers and those who still do not know God.

CHRISTIAN WORKERS

He will rescue us because you
are helping by praying for us.

2 CORINTHIANS 1:11

There are multitudes of Christian workers ministering in connection with our churches and missions, schools and colleges, our publishers and bookstores, our public service and government offices, young men and young women, children and youth, our worship in music, our military personnel, hospitals and clinics, prisons, and our poor. Praise God for this! How much more they could accomplish if each were living in the fullness of the Holy Spirit! Pray for them; it makes you a partner in their work. You will praise God each time you hear of blessings anywhere.

Pray with definite requests. Jesus asked the blind beggar, "What do you want me to do for you?" (Luke 18:41). The Lord knew what the man wanted, and yet He asked him. Verbalizing our wish gives meaning to our transaction with God. It awakens faith and expectation.

Being definite in your requests also helps you to know what answer you are looking for. Ask those you are praying for what they need. If they have prayer letters, use them as guides. Intercession is not mere words and pious wishes. Its aim is to receive and bring down blessing through believing, persevering prayer.

MISSION WORK

One day as these men were worshiping the *Lord*
and fasting, the *Holy Spirit* said, "*Dedicate* Barnabas
and Saul for the special work I have for them."

ACTS 13:2

The evangelization of the world depends, first of all, upon a revival of prayer. The need for the forgotten secret of prevailing, worldwide prayer is greater than the need for missionaries.

Pray that our missions work may all be done in this spirit: waiting on God, hearing the voice of the Spirit, sending out men and women with fasting and prayer. Pray that in our churches our mission interests may be in the power of the Holy Spirit and of prayer. It is a Spirit-filled, praying church that will send out Spirit-filled missionaries, mighty in prayer.

Take time when you pray. The psalmist said, "I give my-self unto prayer" (Psalm 109:4 KJV). The early church leaders agreed. "We can spend our time in prayer" (Acts 6:4). Solomon in his God-given wisdom said, "Don't make rash promises to God. . . . Let your words be few" (Ecclesiastes 5:2).

Time is one of the main standards to measure value. The time we give is proof of the interest we feel. We need time with God—to know His presence and to wait for Him to make Him-self known. We need time to consider and feel the needs we pray for. We need time to pray until we can believe that we have received.

SCHOOLS AND COLLEGES

*"These words I have given you. . .will be on
your lips and on the lips of your children
and your children's children forever."*

ISAIAH 59:21

The future of the Church and the world depends on today's education. The Church may be seeking to evangelize unbelievers but is giving up her own children to secular and materialistic influences. Pray for schools and colleges and for godly teachers. The Church also has a duty to care for its children.

Do not limit God in your prayers. It is a fearful thing to do so. "They tested God's patience and frustrated the Holy One of Israel" (Psalm 78:41). Jesus "did only a few miracles there because of their unbelief" (Matthew 13:58). However, apart from such unbelief, God is not limited. "Is anything too hard for the LORD?" (Genesis 18:14). "O Sovereign LORD! You have made the heavens and earth by your great power. Nothing is too hard for you! . . . I am the LORD. . . . Is anything too hard for me?" (Jeremiah 32:17, 27).

Beware of limiting God in your prayer, not only by unbelief but also by pretending that you know what He can do. Expect unexpected things, greater than all we ask or think. Each time you intercede, be quiet first and worship God. Acknowledge what He can do and expect great things.

SUNDAY SCHOOLS

"The captives of warriors will be released, and the plunder
of tyrants will be retrieved. For *I* will fight those
who fight you, and I will save your children."

ISAIAH 49:25

Every part of the work of God's Church is His work. He must do it. Prayer is acknowledging that He will. It is the surrender of ourselves into His hands to let Him work in us and through us. Pray for hundreds of thousands of Sunday school teachers who know God that they may be filled with His Spirit. Pray for your own Sunday school. Pray for the salvation of the children.

Pray boldly. "We have a great High Priest. . .Jesus the Son of God. . . . So let us come boldly to the throne of our gracious God" (Hebrews 4:14, 16).

As we have been thinking about the work of intercession, what is it doing for us? Does it make us aware of our weakness in prayer? Thank God for this. It is the very first lesson we need on the way to praying the "earnest prayer of a righteous person [that] has great power and wonderful results" (James 5:16). Let us persevere taking each item boldly to the throne of grace.

As we pray, we shall learn to pray, to believe, and to expect with increasing boldness. Hold fast your confidence; it is at God's command you come as an intercessor. Christ will give you grace to pray as you should.

THE MISTAKE

Remain in *me*,
and *I* will remain in you.

JOHN 15:4

A person thinks, I have my business, family, and community responsibilities. In addition I am to serve God in order to keep from sin. I hope God will help me.

That is not right. When Christ came He bought you with His blood. In those days there was slavery. If someone bought a slave, the slave was required to take orders from his master. The slave lived as if he had no will or interests of his own. His one responsibility was to promote the well-being of his master.

In a similar manner, I have been purchased with the blood of Christ. I am to live every day with one thought, "How can I please my Master?"

We find the Christian life so difficult because we seek for God's blessing while we live life according to our own desires. We make our own plans and choose our own work. Then we ask the Lord to help us not to go too far wrong. Instead, our relationship with Jesus should be that we are entirely at His disposal. We should ask Him daily, "Lord, is there anything in me that is not according to Your will, that is not entirely surrendered to You?"

If we will wait patiently for His guidance there will spring up a relationship between us and Christ so close that we will be amazed. He will take actual possession of us and give us unbroken fellowship.

THE UNREACHED

"See, my people will return from
far away, from. . .as far south as Egypt."

ISAIAH 49:12

Will the unreached come to Christ? Does God have such a plan? "Let Egypt come with gifts of precious metals; let Ethiopia bow in submission to God" (Psalm 68:31). "I, the LORD, will bring all to pass at the right time" (Isaiah 60:22).

Pray for those who are yet without the Word: China with her hundreds of millions without Christ; India with its millions; millions each year living in darkness. If Christ gave His life for them, you can give yourself up to intercede for them.

If you have not started to intercede, begin now. God's Spirit will draw you on. Persevere, however hesitant you are. Ask God to give you some country or people group to pray for. Can anything be nobler than to do as Christ did—to give your life for the unreached?

Pray with confident expectation of an answer. "Ask me and I will tell you some remarkable secrets about what is going to happen here" (Jeremiah 33:3). "This is what the Sovereign LORD says: I am ready to hear Israel's prayers. . .and I am ready to grant them their requests" (Ezekiel 36:37). Both texts refer to promises definitely made, but their fulfillment would depend upon prayer.

THE SUFFERING

Share the sorrow of those being mistreated,
as though you *feel* their pain in your own bodies.

HEBREWS 13:3

We live in a world of suffering! The persecuted believers in Islamic countries, the famine-stricken millions, those in poverty and wretchedness, refugees from armed conflict—and so much more. In our smaller circles, in thousands of homes and hearts, there is great sorrow! In our own neighborhood, how many need help or comfort? Let us have a heart for the suffering. Jesus sacrificed all and identified Himself with our suffering! Let us in our measure do so, too. It will stir us to pray, to work, to hope, to love more. And in a way and time we do not understand, God will hear our prayers.

Pray always without giving up. "Jesus told his disciples a story to illustrate their need for constant prayer and to show them that they must never give up" (Luke 18:1).

Have you begun to feel that prayer is really the help needed for this sinful world? The very greatness of the task makes us despair! What can our ten minutes of intercession accomplish? It is okay that we feel this: It may be the way in which God is calling and preparing us to give more of our time to prayer. Give yourself wholly to God, pour out your heart to others in love, and look to God in dependence and expectation. To a heart thus led by the Holy Spirit, it is possible to pray always and not give up.

THE SPIRIT IN YOUR OWN WORK

I *work* very hard at this, as I *depend* on Christ's
mighty power that works within me.

COLOSSIANS 4:29

You have your own special work; make it a work of intercession. Paul worked hard, depending on God's power working
in him. Remember, God not only created us but works in us.
You can do your work only in His strength—by Him working
in you through the Spirit.

Intercede often for those you work with and for other believers, too. Pray in God's very presence. "Draw close to God,
and God will draw close to you" (James 4:8).

The nearness of God gives rest and power in prayer. The
nearness of God is given to those who make it their first aim
to "draw close to God." Seek His nearness, and He will give
it. "He will draw close to you." Then it becomes easy to pray
in faith.

Remember that when first God takes you into the school
of intercession, it is almost more for your own sake than that
of others. You have to be trained to love and wait and pray
and believe. Only persevere. Learn to place yourself in His
presence, to wait quietly for the assurance that He draws near.
Enter His holy presence, wait there, and bring your concerns
before Him.

THE LOCAL CHURCH

Beginning in Jerusalem.

LUKE 24:47

Most of us are connected with some church congregation—a community of believers. They are to us the part of Christ's body with which we come into most direct contact. They have a special claim on our intercession. Let it be a settled matter between God and you that you are to intercede on their behalf.

Pray for the minister and all leaders and workers. Pray for the believers according to their needs. Pray for conversions. Pray for the power of the Spirit to manifest itself. Join with others in specific prayer. Let intercession be a definite work, carried on as systematically as preaching or Bible studies. And pray, expecting an answer.

Pray continually. Read the scriptures. "Watchmen. . . will pray to the LORD day and night. . . . Take no rest, all you who pray" (Isaiah 62:6). ". . .His chosen people who plead with him day and night" (Luke 18:7). "Night and day we pray earnestly for you" (1 Thessalonians 3:10). "But a woman who is a true widow, one who is truly alone in this world, has placed her hope in God. Night and day she asks God for help and spends much time in prayer" (1 Timothy 5:5).

When the glory of God and the love of Christ and the needs of others are revealed to us, the fire of this unceasing intercession will begin to burn in us for those who are near and those who are far away.

THE SALVATION OF SOULS

Therefore *he* is able, once and forever, to save
everyone who comes to God through *him*. *He lives*
forever to plead with God on their behalf.

HEBREWS 7:25

Christ's power to save depends on unceasing intercession. "Then we can spend our time in prayer and preaching and teaching the word. . . . God's message was preached in ever-widening circles. The number of believers greatly increased" (Acts 6:4, 7). After the apostles spent time away in continual prayer, the number of the disciples multiplied greatly.

As we spend time in intercession, we will see more conversions. Christ is exalted as sinners repent. The Church exists with the divine purpose and promise of conversions. Don't be ashamed to confess our sin and weakness and pray to God for more conversions both here and in other countries. Plead for the salvation of sinners.

Pray in deep humility. "Yes, Lord. . .but even dogs are permitted to eat crumbs. . . . Woman. . .your faith is great. Your request is granted" (Matthew 15:27–28).

True humility proves its integrity by not seeking for anything but simply trusting His grace. And so it is the strength of a great faith. Don't let your littleness hinder you for a moment.

YOUNG CONVERTS

As soon as {Peter and John} arrived, they *prayed*
for these new Christians to receive the *Holy Spirit*.
The *Holy Spirit* had not yet come upon any of them.

ACTS 8:15–16

Many new converts remain weak, many fall into sin, and many backslide entirely. As you pray for the Church, its growth in holiness and devotion to God, pray especially for the young converts. Many stand alone, surrounded by temptation. Many have no teaching on the Spirit in them and the power of God to establish them. They don't know the promise of scripture: "It is God who gives us, along with you, the ability to stand firm for Christ. . . . He has identified us as his own by placing the Holy Spirit in our hearts" (2 Corinthians 1:21–22). Many are in other countries, surrounded by Satan's power.

Pray for the power of the Spirit in the Church and especially that every young convert may know the fullness of the Spirit. Pray without ceasing.

"As for me, I will certainly not sin against the LORD by ending my prayers for you" (1 Samuel 12:23). It is sin against the Lord to stop praying for others. Once we begin to see how indispensable intercession is—just as much a duty as loving God—we will feel that to stop intercession is sin.

Ask for grace to fill the role of intercessor with joy and give our life to bring down the blessings of heaven.

THE SPIRIT OF INTERCESSION

*"I chose you. I appointed you to go and
produce fruit. . .so that the Father will give
you whatever you ask for, using my name."*

JOHN 15:16

Often our intercession lacks power because we have not prayed
in the name of Jesus. He promised His disciples that when the
Holy Spirit came upon them, they could ask for anything in
His name.

Let us intercede today for all God's children that Christ
may teach them that the Holy Spirit is in them. May He teach
us what it is to live in His fullness and to yield ourselves to
His work of intercession within us. The Church and the world
need nothing as much as a mighty Spirit of intercession to bring
down the power of God on earth. Pray for the Spirit of intercession to bring a great prayer revival.

Pray, joined to Christ. "If you stay joined to me and my
words remain in you, you mall ask any request you like, and it
will be granted!" (John 15:7).

Our acceptance with God—our access to Him—is all in
Christ. As we consciously abide in Him we have the liberty to
ask what we will in the power of the new nature, and it will be
done.

THE WORD OF GOD

It was not only with words but also with power,
for the *Holy Spirit* gave you full assurance
that what we said was true.

1 THESSALONIANS 4:5

Many Bibles are being circulated. Many sermons on the Bible are being preached. Many Bibles are being read. The blessing comes not just in words only. The blessing and power comes in the Holy Spirit, when it is preached with the Holy Spirit. "This Good News has been announced by those who preached to you in the power of the Holy Spirit sent from heaven" (1 Peter 1:12).

Pray for the power of the Spirit through the Word in all the world wherever it is being read or heard. Let every mention of the Word of God call us to intercession.

Be alert and pray. "Devote yourselves to prayer with an alert mind and a thankful heart. Don't forget to pray for us, too, that God will give us many opportunities to preach" (Colossians 4:2–3).

Do you see how everything depends upon God and prayer? As long as He lives and loves and hears and works, as long as there are hearts closed to the Word, as long as there is work to be done in carrying the Word—pray at all times.

CHRIST IN HIS PEOPLE

"Yes, *I* am the vine; you are the branches. . . .
But if you stay joined to *me* and *my* words
remain in you, you may ask any request
you like, and it will be granted."

JOHN 15:5, 7

As branches we are to be so like the vine, so entirely identified with it, that everyone may see that we have the same nature and life and spirit. When we pray for the Spirit, let us not only think of a Spirit of power, but the very attitude of Christ Jesus. Ask and expect nothing less for yourself and all God's children.

What must we be or do that will enable us to pray as we should and to receive what we ask? The answer is this: It is the branch life that gives power for prayer. We are branches of Christ, the living vine. We must simply live like branches and abide in Christ; then we shall ask what we will and it shall be done for us.

Struggle in prayer. "Join me in my struggle by praying to God for me" (Romans 15:30). "I want you to know how much I have agonized for you" (Colossians 2:1).

All the powers of evil seek to hinder us in prayer. Prayer is a conflict with opposing forces. It needs our whole heart and all our strength. May God give us grace to struggle in prayer until we have victory.

OBEDIENCE

"If you love *me*, *obey my* commandments.
And I will ask the Father, and *he* will give you
another Counselor, who will never leave you."

JOHN 14:15-16

We have learned how the disciples were trained for the baptism of the Spirit. We have seen what was needed for them to continue with one accord in prayer for the power of the Spirit. Christ was everything to them—even before the cross, but much more after it. With the Resurrection He was their life, their one thought, their only desire.

Was this something special just for the disciples? Or is it something that the Lord asks from all who desire to be filled with the Spirit? God expects it of all His children. The Lord has need of people now as much as then, to receive His Spirit and His power, to minister here on earth and, as intercessors, to link the world to the throne of God.

Is Christ something, nothing, or everything to us? For the average Christian, Christ is something; for the true Christian, Christ is all. When we pray for the power of the Spirit, we must say: "I yield myself with my whole heart to the leading of the Spirit." Full surrender is the question of life or death—an absolute necessity.

THE POWER FROM ON HIGH

"But stay here. . .until the *Holy Spirit* comes
and *fills* you with power from heaven."

LUKE 24:49

The Lord said to the disciples: "Apart from me you can do nothing" (John 15:5). Why is it that He chose these weak men to go out to conquer the world for Him? It was so they would yield themselves to Him and give Him the opportunity to show His power working through them. As the Father had done all the work in Christ when He was on earth, so Christ would now be the great worker, proving in the disciples the power that had been given to Him in heaven and on earth. Their place would be to pray, to believe, and to yield themselves to the mighty power of Christ.

The Holy Spirit would not be in them a power they could possess, but He would possess them. Their work really would be the work of the almighty Christ. Their whole posture would be that of unceasing dependence and prayer and of confident expectation.

The Apostles had learned to know Christ intimately. They had seen His mighty works; they had received His teaching; they had gone with Him through His sufferings. And they had known Him in the power of His Resurrection. They had experienced that resurrection life in their own hearts. Yet they were not capable of making Him known as they should until He Himself had taken possession of them by His Spirit dwelling in them.

Everything calls the Christian to be content with nothing less than the indwelling life and power of the Holy Spirit.

The First Prayer Meeting

They all met together continually for prayer,
along with Mary the mother of Jesus,
several other women, and the brothers of Jesus.

ACTS 1:14

Another mark of the early Church—waiting on the promise of the Father in united prayer.

It is difficult to adequately understand the enormous importance of this first prayer meeting, a prayer meeting which was the simple fulfilling of the command of Christ. It was the first example of the one condition on which His Spirit would be known in power. In it we have the secret key that opens the storehouse of heaven.

Christ had prayed that the disciples might be one, even as He and the Father were one, so the world would know that God loved them as He loved Christ. The disciples were far from such a state when Christ prayed the prayer. We see it in the conflict among them at the Last Supper as to who would be chief.

It was only after Christ had gone to heaven that they would spend ten days in united prayer and be brought to that place of love and purpose which would make them the unified Body of Christ, prepared to receive the Spirit in all His power. What a prayer meeting! The fruit of Christ's training during His three years with them was evident there.

This prayer meeting gives us the law of the kingdom. Where Christ's disciples are linked to each other in love and yield themselves completely to Him, the Spirit will be given from heaven to show God's approval. Christ will show His mighty power.

THE UNITY OF THE SPIRIT

Always keep yourselves united in the Holy Spirit. . . .
We are all one body, we have the same Spirit.

EPHESIANS 4:3-4

We learn from Paul how the Christian communities in different places ought to remember each other in the fellowship of prayer. He writes more than once of how the ministry of intercession glorifies God.

Today there still is a great need for Christians to be drawn close together in the awareness of their being chosen by God. We need to understand our role as a holy priesthood ministering continually the sacrifice of praise and prayer. What can be done to foster the unity of the Spirit?

Nothing will help so much as the separation to a life of more prayer, praying specifically that God's people will demonstrate their unity in a life of holiness and love. That will be a living testimony to the world of what it means to live for God.

Paul names one of the essential differences between God's people and the world: "Pray at all times and on every occasion in the power of the Holy Spirit. Stay alert and be persistent in your prayers for all Christians everywhere" (Ephesians 6:18).

Earnestly desire to bear this mark of the children of God. Resolve to carry this great distinction of the Christian—a life of intercession. Join with others who are committed to praying down a blessing upon His Church. Don't hesitate to give a quarter of an hour every day for meditation on some promise of God to His Church—and then plead with Him for its fulfillment. Unobservedly, slowly, but surely, you will become one with God's people, and receive the power to pray the prayer that accomplishes much.

UNITY IS STRENGTH

After this prayer. . .they were all
filled with the *Holy Spirit*. . . .All the
believers were of one heart and mind.

ACTS 4:31-32

We see the power of union everywhere in nature. How tiny is a drop of rain as it falls. But when many drops are united in one stream, the power quickly becomes irresistible. Such was the prayer at Pentecost. And our prayer can be like that if we unite all our forces in pleading the promise of the Father. When the world comes in like a flood, it can be overcome in the power of united prayer.

Because of the many mountains in Natal, the streams often flow down with great force. The Zulus join hands when they want to pass through a stream. The leader has a strong stick in the right hand and gives his left hand to some strong man who comes behind him. And so they form a chain and help each other cross the current. When God's people reach out their hands to each other in the spirit of prayer, there will be power to resist the terrible influence that the world can exert. In that unity God's children will have power to triumph with God.

Christ's followers stayed ten days in the upper room until they truly had become one heart. When the Spirit of God descended, He not only filled each individual but took possession of the whole group as the Body of Christ. It is in the fellowship of loving and believing prayer that our hearts can be melted into one. Then we will become strong to believe and to accept what God has promised us.

Prayer in the Name of Christ

"You can ask for anything in *my* name, and *I* will do it, because the work of the Son brings glory to the Father."

JOHN 14:13

The link between our prayers and the work of Christ in heaven is wonderful. Much prayer on earth brings Him much glory in heaven. Little prayer means, as far as we are concerned, little glory to the Father. What an incentive to pray. Our prayer is indispensable to glorifying the Father.

Christ desired that His disciples learn to believe in the power of His name and to benefit from His promise of a sure answer. His desire was so strong that we find the promise repeated seven times. He longs to stir in us a confident faith and to teach us to look upon intercession as the most certain way of bringing glory to God.

If we think that prayer is not easy, we need to remember what Christ told His disciples: when the Holy Spirit came they would have power to pray. He promises us, "Ask, using my name, and you will receive, and you will have abundant joy" (John 16:24), to encourage us to yield ourselves to the control of the Spirit. As we believe in the power of the Spirit, intercession will become to us the joy and strength of our service.

When Paul wrote "Whatever you do or say, let it be as a representative of the Lord Jesus, all the while giving thanks through him to God the Father" (Colossians 3:17), he reminds us how everything in life is to bear the signature of the name of Jesus. As we learn to live in that name, we will pray with the confidence that our prayer in Jesus' name will be answered.

THE POWER OF PRAYER

The earnest prayer of a righteous person
has great power and wonderful results.

JAMES 5:16

Prayer is effective with God. It affects the history of His Church and people. Prayer is the one power the Church can exercise in securing the working of God's omnipotence in the world.

The prayer of a righteous person is powerful and effective. A righteous person lives as the servant of righteousness (see Romans 6:16, 19). The Lord loves the righteous and their prayers have power (see Psalm 66:18–19; 1 John 3:22). When Christ gave His great prayer promises, it was to those who keep His commandments. "If you love me, obey my commandments. And I will ask the Father, and he will give you another Counselor, who will never leave you" (John 14:15–16). "But if you stay joined to me and my words remain in you, you may ask any request you like, and it will be granted!" (John 15:7).

When the righteous commit their whole being to take hold of God, prayer is powerful and effective. As Jacob said: "I will not let you go unless you bless me" (Genesis 32:26).

Then comes the earnest prayer of many righteous people together. When two or three agree, there is the promise of an answer. God will display His power even more when hundreds and thousands unite in earnest prayer.

Prayer and Sacrifice

I want you to know how much I have agonized for you.

Colossians 2:1

People who undertake a great venture have to prepare themselves and direct all their abilities to that end. Likewise, we as Christians need to prepare ourselves to pray just as God's Word tells us to love God: "with all your heart, all your soul, all your strength, and all your mind" (Luke 10:27). This is the law of the kingdom. Prayer needs sacrifice of comfort, of time, of self. Sacrifice is the secret of powerful prayer.

Christ Jesus, the great Intercessor, was an example of sacrifice in prayer. It is written of Him, "When he sees all that is accomplished by his anguish, he will be satisfied. . . . I will give him the honors of one who is mighty and great, because he exposed himself to death" (Isaiah 53:11–12). In Gethsemane "he offered prayers and pleadings, with a loud cry and tears, to the one who could deliver him out of death" (Hebrews 5:7). Prayer is sacrifice. David said: "Accept my prayer as incense offered to you, and my upraised hands as an evening offering [sacrifice]" (Psalm 141:2).

Our prayer receives its worth from being rooted in the sacrifice of Jesus Christ. As He gave up everything in His prayer, "Your will be done," our attitude must always be the offering up of everything to God and His service.

When we are reluctant to make the needful sacrifice in waiting upon God, we lack power in our prayer. Christ—the Christ we trust in, the Christ that lives in us—offered Himself a sacrifice to God. It is as this spirit lives and rules in us that we will receive power to pray the earnest prayer that accomplishes much.

Intercession of the Spirit for Saints

The *Father* who knows all hearts *knows* what
the *Spirit* is saying, for the *Spirit pleads* for us
believers in harmony with *God's* own will.

Romans 8:27

These words shed light on the life of prayer of the saints! We do not know what we should pray for. This often hinders our prayer or hinders the faith that is essential to its success. But here we are told that the Holy Spirit prays for us: "The Spirit pleads for us believers in harmony with God's own will."

What hope this gives us! Where and how does the Spirit pray for the saints? In the heart which does not know what to pray He secretly and effectually prays what is in harmony with the will of God. This of course implies that we trust Him to do His work in us and that we spend time with God even when we do not know what to pray.

What a difference it would make in the life of many of God's children if they realized this! We not only have Jesus, the great High Priest, ever living to intercede for us; we not only have the liberty of asking in faith what we desire and the promise that it shall be given to us; but we have in very deed the Holy Spirit to intercede for us in harmony with the will of God.

This calls us to separate ourselves from the world and to yield ourselves wholeheartedly to the leading and praying of the Spirit within us!

ONE WITH ALL BELIEVERS

"I in them and you in me, all being perfected into one. Then the world will know that *you* sent *me* and will understand that *you love* them as much as *you love me."*

JOHN 17:23

The Lord Jesus entrusted these words to us so that we would make them the object of our persistent intercession. Only that would enable us to carry out the last command which He gave: that we should love our brothers and sisters in Christ as He loved us so that our joy would be full.

Our churches today are not always marked by a fervent, affectionate love for all the saints of whatever name or denomination. As a part of our daily fellowship with God, let us pray "that we may be one."

It would be simple if once we connected the words, "our Father," with all the children of God throughout the world. Each time we used the words we would only have to expand this little word "our" into all the largeness of God's Father-love. Just as we say "Father" with the thought of our love to Him, we can say "our" with the childlike affection for all the saints whoever and wherever they be. The prayer that "we may be one" would then bring joy and strength, a deeper bond of fellowship with Christ Jesus and all His saints, and an offering of sweet savor to the Father of love.

THE DISCIPLES' PRAYER

They all met together continually for prayer.

ACTS 4:14

What a lesson it would be to us in the school of prayer to have a clear understanding of what continually meeting for prayer meant to the disciples.

The disciples knew from the words of Jesus that "it is actually best for you that I go away, because if I don't, the Counselor won't come" (John 16:7). They knew that the Spirit would give the glorified Christ to their hearts in a way they had never known Him before. It would be He Himself, in the mighty power of God's Spirit, who would be their strength for the work to which He had called them.

With strong confidence they expected the fulfillment of the promise. Had not the Master given them the assurance of what He would send to them from the throne of the Father in heaven? The disciples prayed with intensity and persistence in the full assurance that, however long the answer might be delayed, He would most assuredly fulfill their desires. Let us realize that the very same promise that was given to the disciples is given to us. Even though we have to cry day and night to God, we can count on the Father to answer our prayers.

As believers we also may unite as one in presenting our requests, even though we cannot be together in one place. We can claim the promise that we, too, will be filled with the Holy Spirit.

PAUL'S REQUEST FOR PRAYER

And *pray* for me, too. *Ask* God to give me the
right words as I boldly *explain* God's secret plan. . .
pray that I will keep on speaking boldly for *him*,
as I should.

EPHESIANS 6:19–20

These words, "pray for me, too," indicate Paul's faith in the absolute necessity and the wonderful power of prayer. Listen to how he asks them to pray: "But pray that I will keep on speaking boldly for him, as I should." Paul had been a minister of the Gospel for more than twenty years. You would think that he had such experience that it would come naturally for him to speak boldly. But his conviction of his own weakness is so deep and his dependence on divine power is so absolute, that he feels he cannot do the work as it should be done without the direct help of God. His total dependence upon God is the ground of all his confidence.

But there is more. Because of his deep spiritual insight into the unity of the Body of Christ, and because of his own dependence on the prayers of others, he pleads for their prayers in the Spirit. Paul could not do without the prayers of the believers.

May we realize anew that Christ is our Intercessor in heaven, and all saints here on earth are engaged in one mighty contest. We must cultivate the gift of unceasing prayer for the power of God's Spirit in all His servants.

Prayer for All Saints

Devote yourselves to prayer with an alert mind and a thankful heart. Don't forget to pray for us, too.

Colossians 4:2–3

Prayer for all saints—it will take time, thought, and love to realize what is included in that expression. It means thinking of the saints you know, thinking of your whole country, thinking of the nations of the world and the saints to be found in each of them, and thinking of the saints of God living in persecuted places. All of these have different circumstances and varying needs for God's help.

Pray for many of God's saints who are walking in the dark because of ignorance or laziness or an evil heart. Think of so many who are in earnest and yet conscious of a life of failure, with little or no power to please God or to serve others. Then think of those whose one aim is to serve the Lord and to be light to those around them. Think of them especially as joining in pleading for the great promise of the Holy Spirit and the love and unity which He alone can give.

This is not the work of one day or one night. It needs a heart which will commit to do serious intercession for the Body of Christ. Once we begin we will find abundant reason for persevering in praying for the love of God to fill the hearts of His people and for the power of the Holy Spirit to accomplish God's work in this world.

Every Day

"Give us our food day by day."

Luke 11:3

There are some Christians who are afraid to promise to pray every day. They believe it is beyond them, and yet they pray to God to give them their food day by day. If a child of God has yielded his whole life to God's love and service, he should count it a privilege to come into God's presence every day.

There are many of us who desire to live wholly for God. We acknowledge that Christ gave Himself for us and that He watches over us without ceasing. We admit that the measure of the love of Christ for us is to be the measure of our love for Him. We want to devote our lives to Christ's kingdom and to the prayer that can bring down God's blessing.

Our invitation to pray day and night for His power on His people and on this needy world may come as a new and unexpected opportunity. Think of the privilege of being allowed to plead every day with God on behalf of His saints for the outpouring of His Spirit and for the coming of His kingdom. If you have not understood the privilege and solemn duty of waiting on God in prayer, the invitation will be most welcome.

A Personal Call

We learned not to rely on ourselves,
but on *God* who can raise the dead.

2 Corinthians 4:9

When we plead with Christians to pray without ceasing there are a large number who quietly decide that such a life is not possible for them. They think they do not have any special gift for prayer. They may not have an intense desire for glorifying Christ in the salvation of souls; they have not yet learned to live not for themselves but for Him who died and rose again for them.

And yet to them we bring the call to offer themselves to live entirely for Christ. We ask them whether they are not ashamed of the selfish life that simply uses Christ as a convenient escape from hell and to secure a place in heaven. We come to them with the assurance that God can change their lives and fill their hearts with Christ and His Holy Spirit. We plead with them to believe that with God all things are possible. He is eager to restore them to the joy of the Father's presence and service.

One step to accomplish this is to listen to the call to live in the power of Christ's abiding presence and in the spirit of unceasing prayer. This is nothing less than a duty, a sacrifice that Christ's love has a right to claim.

The person who accepts the call and draws near to God in humble prayer for the needed grace will have taken the first step to the path that leads to fellowship with God. It will lead to a new faith in Christ Jesus and to a prayer life that will help bring Pentecost again into the hearts of God's people.

ABSOLUTE DEPENDENCE

"Yes, I am the vine; you are the branches. . . .
For apart from *me* you can do nothing."

JOHN 15:5

The Christian life is a life of absolute dependence. At Hampton Court there was a vine that sometimes bore a couple thousand clusters of grapes. People were amazed at its productivity. Later the secret was discovered. Not too far from Hampton Court flows the River Thames. The vine had stretched its roots hundreds of yards under the ground until it came to the riverbed. There, in all the nutrients of the river bottom, it found rich nourishment and moisture. The roots drew the sap all that distance to the branches.

The vine had the work to do. The branches simply had to depend upon the vine and receive what it gave.

That is exactly what Christ desires you to understand. Christ desires that in all your work, the very foundation should be the simple acceptance that Christ must care for all. As you depend on Him He supplies your needs by sending down the Holy Spirit. Jesus wants you to be dependent as you serve Him. Day by day, hour by hour, in everything you do, simply abide before Him. Live in the total helplessness of one who can do nothing.

Absolute dependence upon God is the secret of power in work. You and I have nothing unless we receive it from Jesus.

HUMILITY

"If you want to be *my* follower you must
love me more than your own father and mother,
wife and children, brothers and sisters—
yes, more than your own life."

LUKE 14:26

The gifts of human learning and wisdom often assert themselves in Christians, instead of that entire dependence upon the Holy Spirit of which Christ spoke. Exaltation of self is the consequence. The Church demonstrates the difference between pride in the power of human learning and humility with absolute dependence on the teaching of the Holy Spirit. Without humility we become self-sufficient and cease from persevering in prayer.

Our minds, by the Fall, are self-sufficient and require self-denial. We need to know two things: 1) Our salvation consists of being saved from ourselves or from that which we are by nature; 2) this salvation was given to us in great humility by God, who manifested Himself in human form. The first stipulation of this Savior to fallen man is: "If you want to be my follower you must love me more than. . .your own life." To show that this is only the beginning of man's salvation, Jesus also says: "Let me teach you, because I am humble and gentle, and you will find rest for your souls" (Matthew 11:29).

What a light is here for those who love the light. Self is the whole evil of the fallen nature; self-denial enables us to become a follower of Jesus, our example of humility.

THE KINGDOM OF SELF

The law no longer *holds* you in its power,
because you *died* to its power when you
died with *Christ* on the cross.

ROMANS 7:4

Mankind has fallen from a life in God into a life of self—a life of self-love, self-esteem, and self-seeking. God's creatures chose to concentrate on the perishing pleasures of the world. All sin, death, and hell are nothing else but this kingdom of self.

On the Day of Pentecost a new dispensation of God came forth. On God's part it was the operation of the Holy Spirit in gifts and graces upon the Church. On our part it was the adoration of God in spirit and in truth. All this was to make way for the continual operation of God to enable us, baptized with the Holy Spirit, to absolutely renounce self. We are to use our minds and all the outward things of the world only as enlightened and inspired by the Holy Spirit.

The kingdom of self is the fall of man and the great apostasy from the life of God. The kingdom of Christ is the Spirit and power of God manifesting itself in the birth of a new inward person. When the call of God to repentance comes in your soul, be quiet before God in prayer and humbly attentive to the new life within you. Disregard the workings of your own will and reason. Then you will know the power and love of God in its fullness.

PRAYER: A STATE OF THE HEART

Everything else is worthless when compared with the priceless gain of knowing Christ Jesus my Lord.

PHILIPPIANS 3:8

Jesus, though He had all wisdom, only gave us a small number of moral teachings. This is because He knew that the desire of our hearts is focused on this world. Nothing can set us right but turning the desire of our hearts to God. Therefore He calls us to a total denial of ourselves and the life of this world. He calls us to a faith in Him as the one who gives a new birth and a new life. He teaches us every reason for renouncing ourselves and for loving our redemption as the greatest joy and desire of our heart.

We see that our will and our heart are everything. True religion is only the religion of the heart. We see that a spirit of longing after the life of this world made us the poor pilgrims on earth that we are. Only the spirit of prayer, or the longing desire of the heart after Christ and God and heaven, breaks our bondage and lifts us out of the miseries of time into the riches of eternity.

When the spirit of prayer is born in us, it is no longer confined to a certain hour but is the continual breathing of the heart after God. The spirit of prayer, as a state of the heart, becomes the governing principle of the soul's life.

A Continual Relationship

Don't worry about anything;
instead, *pray* about everything.

PHILIPPIANS 4:6

Seeing and knowing our selfish condition calls us to prayer. The desire of our heart becomes the spirit of prayer. What characteristics of prayer should distinguish the Christian?

At times an honest person may show honesty by actions. At other times there is no special situation to confirm this honesty. But honesty is, all the same, the inward living principle of that person's heart. Just so the spirit of prayer may quietly possess the heart without interruption and at other times may have certain hours of prayer. But prayer that has its own life and spirit is vastly superior to any ritual form. It is independent and has no particular hours or forms of work.

It would be worthwhile to study the place that the word "continual" ought to have in our life: continual joy of the infinite love of God toward us; continual unalterable dependence upon God every hour of our life; the continual receiving of goodness and happiness from God alone; the continual denial of our evil nature; the continual and immediate inspiration of the Holy Spirit maintaining the life of Christ in us; the continual breathing of the heart after God in prayer; and then the continual loving Him with our whole heart.

THE TOUCHSTONE OF TRUTH

God sets *himself* against the proud,
but *he shows* favor to the humble.

JAMES 4:6

There is an infallible touchstone that will teach you the spirit of prayer. Pull away from the world and all activities. Stop the former workings of your heart and mind. With all your strength, spend all this month as continually as you can in one kind of prayer to God. Offer it frequently on your knees but, whether sitting, standing, or walking, always be inwardly longing and earnestly praying this one prayer to God.

Pray that He would show you and take from your heart every form of pride. Pray that He would awaken in you the depths of humility so that you will be open to His light and His Holy Spirit. Reject every thought except that of praying in this matter from the bottom of your heart.

The painful sense and feeling of what you are, kindled by the light of God within you, is the fire and light from which your spirit of prayer proceeds. At first nothing is found or felt but pain and darkness. But as this prayer of humility is met by the divine love, the mercy of God embraces it. Then your prayer is changed into songs and thanksgiving.

THE STEP OF PRAYER

Keep on *praying*.

1 THESSALONIANS 5:17

If you have already taken the first step in the spiritual life, you have devoted yourself absolutely to God to live wholly for His will. You have chosen to be under the light and guidance of His Holy Spirit.

The next step is to continually give yourself to God. This second step cannot be taken except by prayer. Nothing else has power here but prayer. This prayer must come from your heart and your relationship with God. Consider this prayer an infallible guide to heaven. As a person who has some great responsibility turns from everything that is not related to it, so your heart will focus on its own state of prayer as soon as God is its objective.

Our times of prayer are meant to lead us on to a life of prayer. Just as the eye can rejoice all the day in the sunshine which gives it light, so the heart will continually live and rejoice in God's presence. Let us believe that God, who is able to do exceeding abundantly above all that we ask or think, is indeed able and willing to lead us into a life of prayer. By the power of His Holy Spirit, He will strengthen us for this life of unceasing prayer as we walk in the light of His countenance.

The Love of God

*"And you must love the LORD your God with all your heart,
all your soul, and all your strength."*

DEUTERONOMY 6:5

Moses taught Israel what the first and great commandment was: to love God with all their heart. It has its foundation in the relationship between God as the loving Creator and His creation as the object of that love. People find their life, destiny, and happiness as they love God with all their heart and strength.

Moses said that, "The LORD chose your ancestors as the objects of his love" (Deuteronomy 10:15). Such a God was infinitely worthy of being loved. All our faith in God and obedience to Him is to be inspired by this one thought: We are to love God with all our heart and all our strength. Every day our first duty should be to live out this command.

How little Israel was able to obey the command we all know so well. This is true of us even today. We are content in the thought that such love is impossible for us to produce. We forget that it is the Holy Spirit that enables us to love God and walk in His ways.

A perfect heart that loves God is what He claims and what He is completely worthy of. As we pray, expect the fulfillment of God's promises as we love Him with our whole heart.

THE THOUGHTS OF GOD

*"For just as the heavens are higher than the earth,
so are my thoughts higher than your thoughts."*

ISAIAH 55:9

God reminds us that as high as the heavens are above the earth, so high His thoughts are above ours. They are altogether beyond the power of our comprehension. When God laid out all His promises to Abraham, they were indeed thoughts higher than the heavens.

God tells us that we are made in His image. By grace we are actually renewed again into that image. As we gaze upon God's glory in Christ, we are changed into the same image by His Spirit. These, too, are thoughts beyond our comprehension—our minds cannot take them in.

God, by His Holy Spirit, conveys to our hearts the life and the light that can make us feel at home with these thoughts dwelling in us. But we need daily, prayerful fellowship with God if we are to enter into His mind and to have His thoughts make their home in us. It is by faith that God will not only reveal the beauty and the glory of these thoughts but will actually work in us their divine reality.

Just think of what Paul writes: "'No eye has seen, no ear has heard, and no mind has imagined what God has prepared for those who love him'" (1 Corinthians 2:9). But as we pray God will reveal them through His Spirit.

THE NEW COVENANT IN HEBREWS

And *I* will forgive their wrongdoings,
and *I* will never again remember their sins.

HEBREWS 8:12

In this Epistle of Hebrews, Christ is called the Mediator of a better covenant, based upon better promises (8:6). In Him the two parts of the covenant find their complete fulfillment. First of all, He came to atone for sin so that its power over man was destroyed. And with that came the fuller blessing—a new heart, with God's Holy Spirit breathing into it delight in God's law and the power to obey it.

These two parts of the covenant may never be separated. There are so many who put their trust in Christ for the forgiveness of sin and yet never think of claiming the fullness of His promised blessings.

Jesus Christ is the Mediator of the new covenant with the forgiveness of sin in the power of His Spirit. Just as surely as complete pardon of sin is assured, the complete fulfillment of God's promises should be expected, too.

To appropriate the new covenant, it requires a strong desire for a life wholly given to Christ. As we pray let us be willing to accept our place with Him—crucified to the world, to sin, and to self. It means a readiness to follow Him at any cost. It means a simple, wholehearted acceptance of Christ as Lord and Master and a surrender of our heart and life to Him.

FAITH IN CHRIST

"You trust God, now trust in me."

JOHN 14:1

When Christ was about to leave His disciples, He taught them that they were to believe in Him with the same perfect confidence with which they had believed in God. "Just believe that I am in the Father. . . . Anyone who believes in me will do the same works I have done" (John 14:11–12). Here on earth He had not been able to make Himself fully known to His disciples. But in heaven, the fullness of God's power would be His. Jesus would do greater things in and through His disciples than He had ever done here on earth.

This faith must focus itself on the person of Christ in His union with the Father. The disciples were to have perfect confidence that all God had done could now be done by Jesus, too. The deity of Christ is the rock on which our faith depends. God's power has worked in Christ through His resurrection from the dead. Christ can also, in His divine power, work in us all that we need.

Take time in prayer to worship Jesus in His divine omnipotence as one with the Father. Bow in deep humility before the Lord Jesus and worship Him as Thomas did: "My Lord and my God!" (John 20:28). Let the Savior you have known and loved become, as never before, the Mighty God. Let Him always be your confidence and your strength.

CHRIST'S LIFE IN US

"For I will live again, and you will, too."

JOHN 14:19

There is a great difference in the teaching of the first three Gospels and that of John. John's special relationship with Jesus allows him to understand the Master better than the others. The others speak of repentance and the pardon of sin as the first great gift of the New Testament, but they say little of the new life in Christ.

It is John who records what Christ taught about His very own life really becoming ours. We are united with Him just as He was with the Father. The other Gospels speak of Christ as the Shepherd seeking and saving the lost. John speaks of Him as the Shepherd who gives His life for the sheep—His very life becoming ours. "My purpose is to give life in all its fullness" (John 10:10).

And so Christ says here in John, "I will live again, and you will, too." The disciples were to receive from Him the resurrection life in the power of its victory over death. From now on He would always dwell in them. This promise applies to all who will accept it in faith.

Take time to pray and let Christ's wonderful promise of a new life take possession of your heart. Be content with nothing less than full salvation—Christ living in you, and you living in Christ.

The Obedience of Love

"When you *obey me*, you remain in *my* love."

JOHN 15:10

The question is often asked: How can I abide in Christ and live wholly for Him? In our text the Lord gives the simple but far-reaching answer: obey Him. This is the only way to remain in Him. "When you obey me, you remain in my love, just as I obey my Father and remain in his love" (John 15:10). Loving obedience is the way to enjoy His love.

In John chapter 15 Jesus frequently connected keeping His commandments with loving Him. "If my words remain in you, you may ask any request you like, and it will be granted" (15:7). "When you obey me, you remain in my love" (15:10). "You are my friends if you obey me" (15:14). The love that keeps His commandments is the only way to remain in His love. In our whole relationship to Christ, love is everything. Christ's love to us and our love to Him is proved in our love to each other.

The power of Christ's life through the Holy Spirit is pledged to those who truly love Him and keep His commands. This is the great secret of remaining in Christ and of having Him dwell in us. Then the divine power of our prayer will bring down God's blessing.

THE PROMISE OF THE SPIRIT

"If I do go away, {the Counselor} will come because I will send him to you. He will bring me glory by revealing to you whatever he receives from me."

JOHN 16:7, 14

From out of the glory of heaven the crucified Christ sent the Holy Spirit into the hearts of His disciples. The Spirit of Christ became their life in fellowship with Him and their power for His service. The Spirit comes to us, too, as the Spirit of the divine glory. We are to welcome Him and yield ourselves absolutely to His leading.

Yes, the Spirit of Christ came to dwell in the disciples and to make them the conscious possessors of the presence of the glorified Christ. It was this Spirit who was their power for a life of loving obedience. He was their teacher and leader in praying down from heaven the blessing that they needed. It was in His power that they conquered God's enemies and carried the Gospel to the ends of the world.

The Spirit is God. As God, He claims to have possession of our whole being. Our heart and life are to be entirely and unceasingly under His control. In prayer we are to be led by the Spirit every day and every hour. In His power our life is to be a direct and continual abiding in the love and fellowship of Jesus. The Spirit who searches the deep things of God claims the very depths of our being and reveals Christ as Lord and Ruler.

IN CHRIST

"When I am raised to life again,
you will know that I am in my Father,
and you are in me, and I am in you."

JOHN 14:20

Our Lord spoke of His life in the Father in John 14:11: "Just believe that I am in the Father and the Father is in me." He and the Father were not two persons next to each other; they were in each other. Even as a man on earth, Jesus lived in the Father. All He did was what the Father did in Him.

This picture of Christ in God and God in Christ is the pledge of what our life in Christ is to be here on earth. We must always live in the faith that we are in Christ and yield ourselves to His power. Then we will learn that, even as the Father worked in Christ, so Christ will also work in us.

As the Father worked in Christ because He lived in the Father, so Christ worked in the disciples as they lived in Him. Their life in Him was the reflection of His life in the Father. But this did not happen until the Holy Spirit came. They had to wait until they were clothed with the power of the Spirit. Then by daily fellowship and prayer He did in them the greater works He had promised.

The secret of our power is to be found in nothing less than where Christ found it—abiding in the Father and His love.

THE POWER OF PRAYER

*"If you stay joined to me and my words
remain in you, you may ask any request
you like, and it will be granted!"*

JOHN 15:7

Before Jesus went to heaven, He taught His disciples two great lessons in regard to their relationship to Him in the work they had to do.

The one was that, in heaven, Jesus would have much more power than He had here on earth. He would now use that power through His disciples for the salvation of men.

The other was that without Him they could do nothing. Their first and chief work would therefore be to bring everything they wanted done to Him in prayer. In His farewell discourse, Jesus repeats the promise seven times: "Remain in me, pray in my name." "Ask any request you like and it will be granted." You can count on it!

With these truths written in their hearts, He sent the disciples out into the world to accomplish His work. The disciples on earth always looked up to Him in prayer, fully confident that He would hear their prayer. The first and only condition is an unflinching confidence in the power of His promise.

The same condition applies for us today. Close, abiding fellowship with Christ begins with deep dependence and unceasing prayer. It is only then that we can do our work in the full assurance that God has heard our prayer and will be our source of strength.

CHRIST OUR RIGHTEOUSNESS

Now *God* in *his* gracious kindness *declares* us not guilty. *He* has done this through *Christ Jesus,*
who has freed us by taking away our sins.

ROMANS 3:24

The first three Gospels speak of redemption as a pardon of sin, or justification. John speaks of it as a life which Christ is to live in us, or regeneration.

In the book of Romans we find both truths in their beautiful connection and harmony. Early in his epistle Paul speaks of justification. But then he goes on from there to speak of the life that we have in our union with Christ. In Romans 4 he tells us that we find both of these truths in the life of Abraham. God first of all counted Abraham's faith as righteousness. Then He empowered him to believe in Him as the God who can give life to the dead.

As believers we know that justification comes at the moment of conversion. But that is only the beginning. Gradually the believer must understand that his calling now is to remain in Christ and to let Christ remain and work in him.

Most Christians have learned from Abraham the first lesson: to believe in God who justifies the ungodly. But they fail to go beyond that because they do not prayerfully yield themselves to Christ to maintain His life in them. The grace of pardon is only the beginning. Growing in grace leads to a fuller experience of what it means to be in Christ, to live in Him, and to grow in Him.

CHRIST OUR LIFE

All who receive *God's* wonderful, gracious gift of righteousness
will live in triumph over sin and
death through this one man *Jesus Christ*.

ROMANS 5:17

Paul teaches that faith in Christ as our righteousness is to be followed by faith in Him as our life from the dead. He now asks:
"Have you forgotten that when we became Christians and were
baptized to become one with Christ Jesus, we died with him?"
(Romans 6:3). We are now to consider ourselves as truly "dead
to sin and able to live for the glory of God" (verse 11).

The new life in us is an actual participation in and experience of the risen life of Christ. Our death to sin in Christ is also
a spiritual reality. It is only when we see how we were one with
Christ on the cross in His death and in His Resurrection that we
will understand that "death no longer has any power over [us]"
(Romans 6:9). This is the true life of faith.

Being in Christ and having Him live His life in us can only
come true as the full power of the Holy Spirit is experienced.
Paul says in Romans 8:2 that "The power of the life-giving Spirit
has freed you through Christ Jesus from the power of sin that
leads to death." And he then adds: "that the requirement of the
law would be fully accomplished for us who no longer follow
our sinful nature but instead follow the Spirit" (Romans 8:4).
Through the Spirit we enter into the glorious liberty of the children of God.

FULL CONSECRATION

Yes, everything else is worthless when compared with the priceless gain of knowing Christ Jesus my Lord.

PHILIPPIANS 3:8

What was it that made just the disciples worthy of the high honor of being baptized with the Holy Spirit? The answer is simple. When Christ called them they gave up everything and followed Him. They denied themselves and, in obedience, submitted to Christ's commands. They followed Him to Calvary. And even as Christ suffered and died, their hearts clung to Him alone.

Just as Jesus Christ had to sacrifice all to be a perfect offering to God, so we His people must give up everything to follow God's divine leading. This was true for Paul, too. To count all things but loss for Christ was the keynote of his life. It must be ours also if we are to fully share in the power of His Resurrection.

As the merchant who found the treasure in the field had to sell all he had to purchase it, we must relinquish our whole heart, life, and strength in order to claim Christ. It is only then that we can share with Him in His victory through the power of the Holy Spirit. The law of the kingdom is unchangeable; "Everything else is worthless when compared with the priceless gain of knowing Christ Jesus my Lord." It is in this that we find the path to the fullness of the Spirit.

ENTIRE SANCTIFICATION

Now may the God of peace make you holy in every way
. . . God, who calls you, is faithful; he will do this.

1 THESSALONIANS 5:23–24

What a promise! Just listen: God, the God of peace Himself, promises to sanctify us completely in Christ. It is God who is doing the work. It is in close, personal fellowship with God Himself that we become holy.

This should make us rejoice, but it is as if the promise is too great, and so it is repeated and amplified: "Now the God of peace make you holy in every way, and may your whole spirit and soul and body be kept blameless until that day when our Lord Jesus Christ comes again." To prevent the possibility of any misconception, the words are added: "God, who calls you, is faithful; he will do this."

Yes, God has said: "I, the LORD, have spoken! I will do what I have said" (Ezekiel 22:14). All that He asks is that we prayerfully stay in close fellowship with Him every day. As the heat of the sun shines on the body and warms it, the fire of God's holiness will burn in us and make us holy.

Child of God, beware of unbelief. It dishonors God; it robs your soul of its heritage. Let every thought of your high and holy calling respond: "God, who calls you, is faithful; he will do this." Yes, He will do it; and He will give you the grace to stay close to Him.

THE EXCEEDING GREATNESS OF HIS POWER

I *pray* for you constantly, asking God. . .to give you spiritual wisdom. . .I *pray* that you will begin to understand the incredible greatness of *his* power.

EPHESIANS 1:16–17, 19

This is one of the great texts that will make our faith strong and bold. Paul was writing to believers who had been sealed with the Holy Spirit. Yet he felt the need to pray for them for the enlightening of the Holy Spirit. They needed to know that it was the mighty power of God that was working in them. It was the very same power by which God raised Christ from the dead.

When Christ died on the cross, He died under the weight of the sin of the world and its curse. When He descended into the grave, it was under the weight of all that sin that He was buried. The power of death had apparently conquered Him. But the mighty power of God raised Christ from the dead to a place of honor at God's right hand.

It is that very same power that is working in us every day of our lives. The God who said to Abraham, "Is anything too hard for the LORD?" (Genesis 18:14), pledges to work His power in us, too, if we will learn to trust Him.

Pray in faith to God and trust His Holy Spirit to enable us to claim nothing less than the exceeding greatness of this Resurrection power working in us.

THE INDWELLING CHRIST

I pray that *Christ* will be more and more at
home in your hearts as you *trust* in *him*.

EPHESIANS 3:17

The great privilege that separated Israel from other nations was this: They had God dwelling in their midst. He made His home in the tabernacle and the temple. In the New Testament we see God dwelling in the heart of the believer. Jesus said: "All those who love me will do what I say. My Father will love them, and we will come to them and live with them" (John 14:23). Or, as Paul says of himself, "Christ lives in me" (Galatians 2:20).

The gospel is the dispensation of the indwelling Christ. In Ephesians 3:14–19 Paul teaches how we can experience this blessing of the Christian life.

1. "I fall on my knees and pray to the Father." The blessing must come from the Father to the praying believer.

2. "I pray that from his glorious, unlimited resources he will give you mighty inner strength through his Holy Spirit."

3. "I pray that Christ will be more and more at home in your hearts as you trust in him." It is in the very nature of Christ to desire to live in the heart of faith.

4. "May your roots go down deep into the soil of God's marvelous love."

Prayerfully meditate on what Christ, through the Holy Spirit, has chosen to do. He has chosen to make His home in our hearts!

CHRISTIAN PERFECTION

And now may the God of peace. . .equip you
with all you need for doing *his* will. May *he*
produce in you. . .all that is pleasing to *him*.

HEBREWS 13:20–21

The book of Hebrews wonderfully explains the redemption that Christ worked out for us in His death. The writer closes his teaching with a benediction. Listen: "The God of peace. . .equip you with all you need for doing his will. May he produce in you. . . all that is pleasing to him." Can we possibly desire more?

All that God has done for our redemption has one purpose: that He might now have free rein to work out in us that redemption which Christ had accomplished. All that we have learned about the completeness of salvation in Christ is consummated in the promise that God Himself will equip us to do what is pleasing in His sight. And this is accomplished through Jesus Christ.

The thought of being totally equipped to please Him is too high; the promise is too large. And yet the promise remains, stimulating our faith. It calls us to take hold of this truth—the everlasting God works in me every hour of the day through Jesus Christ. I have just one thing to do: to yield myself into God's hands for Him to work and not to hinder Him by any of my efforts. In silent prayer and adoring faith, be assured that God Himself will work in us all that is well-pleasing in His sight. Lord, increase our faith!

OVERCOMING THE WORLD

The ones who win this battle against the world
are the ones who believe that *Jesus* is the *Son of God*.

1 JOHN 5:5

Early on in this epistle John teaches us what the real nature and power of the world consists of: the lust for physical pleasure, the lust for everything we see, and pride in our possessions. We find these three marks of the world in the Garden of Eden. Through the body, the eyes, and the pride of wisdom, the world acquired the mastery over Eve and over us. Ever since, the kingdom of God and the kingdom of this world have been in deadly conflict.

The world still exerts a terrible influence over Christians who do not know that in Christ they have been crucified to the world. The power of this world proves itself in all the pleasures of sin. And most Christians are either ignorant of the danger of a worldly spirit or feel utterly powerless to conquer it.

Christ left us with this great far-reaching promise: "But take heart, because I have overcome the world." As we abide in Christ and seek to live a holy life in the power of the Holy Spirit, we may confidently count on that power to overcome the world. "The ones who win this battle against the world are the ones who believe that Jesus is the Son of God." Prayerfully place your trust in the mighty power of God as the only pledge of certain and continual victory.

AUTHOR AND PERFECTER OF OUR FAITH

"I do believe, but help me not to doubt."

What a treasure of encouragement these words from Mark contain. Jesus had said to the father who had asked Him to heal his child: "Anything is possible if a person believes" (Mark 9:23). The father felt that Christ was throwing the responsibility on him. If he believed, the child could be healed. But he felt his faith was totally inadequate. Yet as he looked in the face of Christ, he felt assured that the love which was willing to heal would also be ready to help him with his weak faith. So he cried: "I do believe, but help me not to doubt." Christ heard the prayer, and the child was healed.

Christ will always accept the faith that puts its trust in Him. Remember the mustard seed. If it is put into the ground and allowed to grow, it becomes a great tree. The weakest faith is made strong and bold when it trusts Christ—the Author and Perfecter of our faith.

Take the hidden seed of little faith and plant it in your heart. Rest on God's promise as you bring it to Him in prayer. He will certainly embrace the trembling faith that clings to Him and will not let Him go. A weak faith in an almighty Christ will become the great faith that can remove mountains.

Prayer to Be Holy

Christ will make your hearts strong, blameless,
and holy when you *stand* before *God* our *Father*
on that day when our *Lord Jesus* comes.

1 Thessalonians 3:13

This is a prayer for holiness, which is the very nature of God, inseparable from His being. We are in Christ, who is made of God our sanctification. The Spirit of God is the Spirit of holiness. We have been sanctified in Christ Jesus. The new nature we have from Him has been created in true holiness.

It is as we believe in God, through Christ and the Holy Spirit working in us, that the inflow of the holy life from above is renewed. And as we believe we have the courage and the power to live out that holy life.

Like the whole of salvation, the life of holiness is the result of cooperating with God in faith: First of all, our entire dependence on and surrender to God is the only source of goodness or strength. Then we must act out in life and conduct all that God has worked within us.

Believers, God desires your sanctification. Worship God in His holiness until every thought of God in His glory and grace is connected with the deep conviction that the blessed God wills your holiness. Do not rest until your will has surrendered unconditionally to the will of God and found its true destiny in receiving that divine will and working it out.

WHEN TROUBLE COMES

Patient endurance is what you need now,
so you will continue to do *God's* will.
Then you will receive all that *he* has promised.

HEBREWS 10:36

The first concern of most Christians in trouble is to be delivered from it. However, perhaps this should not be the primary thing. Our one great desire ought to be that we do not fail in knowing or doing the will of God in anything. This is the secret of strength and true character in the Christian life.

When trials come, though, it is beyond human power to think of and do God's will first. It is indeed something beyond human power but not beyond the power of grace. It is just for this that our Lord Jesus came to earth—to do God's will. He went to the cross with the prayer to God: "Not My will, but Yours be done."

Ask God to renew your spirit and your mind and to show you how He would have you live wholly in His will. Yield yourself to that will in everything you know and do it. Yield yourself to that will in all its divine love and quickening power as it works in you and makes you a partaker of its inmost nature. Pray, pray, pray, until you see increasingly in Jesus' life and death the promise and pledge of what God will work in you. Your abiding in Him and your oneness with Him mean nothing less than your being called to do the will of God as He did it.

Humble Praying Rests

"Come to me, all of you who are weary and carry heavy burdens, and I will give you rest."

Matthew 11:28

When Jesus was on earth He did not mention meekness as one of several other virtues that were to be learned from Him, but rather as the one which was His primary characteristic—the one which we must learn if we are to find rest for our souls. He came to deliver us from the sins of self-exaltation and pride.

In heaven He humbled Himself as Son before the Father, that He might be sent as a servant into the world. He humbled Himself to become man. As man He humbled Himself to the death of the cross. He had to come into the world as the gentle Lamb of God to bring to earth the meekness of heart in which true submission to God is manifested.

There is no way to heaven except by meekness, by entirely dying to our pride, and by living entirely in the lowliness of Jesus. Pride gives no rest; it is from hell. It must die or nothing of heaven can live in us. As we come to Him in prayer, God will certainly bestow this meekness and by His Spirit work it out in the heart of everyone who surrenders his life entirely to the power of the blood of the Lamb.

The Spirit works as the Spirit of the Lamb. He works with a hidden but perfect power, breathing into the heart of His own people that which is the divine glory of the Lamb—His meekness.

SILENT LISTENING BEFORE GOD

For we are the temple of the living God.

2 CORINTHIANS 6:16

After worshipping God in prayer with praise and thanksgiving, prepare yourself for intercessory prayer by waiting on God in meditative, prayerful Bible study.

One reason why the discipline of prayer is not attractive is that people do not know how to pray. Their stock of words is soon exhausted, and they do not know what else to say. This happens because they forget that prayer is not a soliloquy where everything comes from one side, but it is a dialogue where God's child listens to what the Father says, replies to it, and then asks for the things he needs.

Read a few verses from the Bible. Do not concern yourself with the difficult parts in them; you can consider these later. Take what you understand, apply it to yourself, and ask the Father to make His Word light and power in your heart. Thus you will have material enough for prayer from the Word which the Father speaks to you. You will also have the liberty to ask for things you need.

Keep on in this way, and prayer will become at length, not a place where you sigh and struggle, but a place of living fellowship with the Father in heaven. Prayerful study of the Bible is indispensable for powerful prayer. The Word prayerfully read and cherished in the heart by faith will, through the Spirit, be both light and life within us.

REQUESTS FOR
WORRISOME NEEDS

*Don't worry about anything; instead,
pray about everything. Tell God what you need,
and thank him for all he has done.*

PHILIPPIANS 4:6

Whenever we come in prayer to present our requests to God, our Lord instructs us to pause long enough to remember who He is: our King, our Righteousness. His Word tells us of His kingdom—the realm in which His servants' requests are to be made.

If we don't acknowledge who He is, prayer is not prayer at all. Instead, the recitation of our worries is simply an attempt to worry God. God is already aware of our needs. He wants us to think over what we ask from Him. Do not be satisfied with going over the same things every day. No child goes on saying the same thing day after day to his earthly father.

Conversation with the Father is colored by the needs of the day. Let your prayer be something definite, rising out of the Word which you have read or out of the real soul—needs which you long to have satisfied. Let your prayer be so definite that you can say, "I know what I have asked for from my Father, and I expect an answer."

It is a good plan sometimes to take a piece of paper and write down what you pray for. You might keep such a paper for a week or more and repeat the prayers until some new need arises.

INTERCESSORY PRAYER

The *Spirit pleads* for us believers
in harmony with *God's* own will.

ROMANS 8:27

After we have humbled ourselves before God in praise and thanksgiving, have received His Word in personal communion with Him, and have made our requests for our own needs, God desires that we continue in prayer as intercessors before Him for the needs of others—to grow in our praying.

Children can ask their father for bread, but full-grown children converse with him about all the interests of his business and other areas of life. Weak children of God pray only for themselves, but persons growing in Christ understand how to consult with God over what must take place in the kingdom. Let your prayer list include the names of those for whom you pray—your minister, and all other ministers, and the different missionary affairs with which you are connected. Thus your prayer time will really become a wonder of God's goodness and a fountain of great joy.

More than one Christian who has desired to give himself to the ministry of intercession has wondered why he has found it so difficult to rejoice in it, to persevere, and to prevail. But we must confess that we have a nature perfectly adapted to do this work God has called us to do. We have been created in Christ to pray. It is our very nature as children of God. God's Spirit has been sent into our hearts to draw our hearts up to God in childlike prayer.

CAREFULLY PRAYING THE WORD

And all who heard *him* {*Jesus*} were amazed
at *his* understanding and *his* answers.

LUKE 2:47

In Jesus' time on earth He treasured the Word in His heart. In the temptation in the wilderness and on every opportunity that presented itself until His death on the cross, He showed that the Word of God filled His heart.

In Jesus' prayer life He manifested two things to us: first, God's Word supplies us with material for prayer and encourages us in expecting everything from God; second, it is only by prayer that we can live such a life so that every word of God can be fulfilled in us.

How can we come to the place where the Word and prayer may each have its undivided right over us? There is only one answer: Our lives must be wholly transformed.

We must, by faith in what God will do in us, appropriate the heavenly life of Christ as He lived it here on earth. We must have the certain expectation that the Spirit, who filled Jesus with the Word and prayer, will also accomplish that work in us.

Let us understand that God the Holy Spirit is essentially the Spirit of the Word and the Spirit of prayer; He is the Spirit of the Lord Jesus who is in us to make us truly partakers of His life. If we firmly believe this and set our hearts upon it, then there will come a change in our use of God's Word and prayer such as we could not have thought possible.

RECEPTIVE PRAYING

The disciples were meeting behind locked doors. . . .
Suddenly, *Jesus* was standing there among them! . . .
*He. . .*said*. . ."Receive* the *Holy Spirit."*

JOHN 20:19, 22

It is foolish to pray for the fullness of the Spirit if we have not first placed ourselves under the full power of the cross! Just think of the disciples. The crucifixion of Christ had touched, broken, and taken possession of their entire hearts. They could speak or think of nothing else, and when the Crucified One had shown them His hands and His feet, He said unto them, "Receive the Holy Spirit."

Christ gave Himself up entirely to the cross. The cross demands this also from us; it would have our entire life. To comply with this demand requires nothing less than a powerful act of the will, for which we are unfit. It also requires a powerful act of God which will assuredly come to those who cast themselves unreservedly on Him.

The Spirit who is in you, in however limited a measure, is prepared to teach you, to lead you to the cross, and to make you know something of what the crucified Christ wills to do for you and in you.

Begin at the beginning. Be faithful in prayer. Although everything appears cold, dark, and strained, bow in silence before the loving Lord Jesus. Thank Him that you can count on Him to meet you there.

Prayer's Obedience of Faith

"But if you stay joined to *me* and *my* words remain in you,
you may ask any request you like, and it will be granted! . . .
When you *obey me*, you remain in *my* love."

JOHN 15:7, 10

If you make the morning hour holy to the Lord, the day with its duties will also be holy.

Do not forget the close bond between the inner chamber and the outer world. The attitude of prayer must remain with us all day. The object of the prayer is to so unite us with God that we may have Him always abiding with us.

Sin, thoughtlessness, and yielding to the flesh or to the world make us unfit for communion with God and bring a cloud over the soul. If you have stumbled or fallen, return to God in prayer. First invoke the blood of Jesus and claim cleansing by it. Do not rest till by confession you have repented of and put away your sin. Let the precious blood really give you a fresh freedom of approach to God.

Remember that the roots of your life in the inner chamber strike far out in body and soul so as to manifest themselves in daily life. Let the obedience of faith, in which you pray in secret, rule you constantly.

The inner chamber is intended to bind us to God, to supply us with power from God, to enable us to live for God alone. Thank God for the inner chamber and for the life which He will enable us to experience and nourish there.

MORNING BY MORNING

Listen to my voice in the morning, *Lord*.
Each morning I *bring* my requests to
you and *wait* expectantly.

Many Christians observe the morning watch, while others speak of it as the quiet hour, the still hour, or the quiet time. All these, whether they think of a whole hour or half an hour or a quarter of an hour, agree with the psalmist.

In speaking of the extreme importance of this daily time of quiet for prayer and meditation on God's Word, a well-known Christian leader has said: "Next to receiving Christ as Savior and claiming the baptism of the Holy Spirit, we know of no act that brings greater good to ourselves or others than the determination to keep the morning watch and spend the first half hour of the day alone with God."

At first glance this statement appears too strong. The firm determination to keep the morning watch hardly appears sufficiently important to be compared to receiving Christ and the baptism of the Holy Spirit. However, it is true that it is impossible to live our daily Christian life, or maintain a walk in the leading and power of the Holy Spirit, without a daily, close fellowship with God. The morning watch is the key to maintaining a position of total surrender to Christ and the Holy Spirit.

We as believers cannot stand for one moment without Christ. Personal devotion to Him refuses to be content with anything less than to abide always in His love and His will. This is the true scriptural Christian life.

NOTHING SEPARATES
US FROM JESUS

*Jesus said, ". . .I do nothing on my own,
but I speak what the Father taught me. And
the one who sent me is with me. . .I always do
those things that are pleasing to him."*

JOHN 8:28-29

The above scripture passage is the beloved apostle John's record of Jesus' unique "personal testimony." It represents the "gold standard" toward which we all should press.

Personal devotion to a friend or a pursuit means that they will always hold a place in our heart, even when other persons and things occupy our attention. Personal devotion to Jesus means that we allow nothing to separate us from Him for a moment. To abide in Him and His love, to be kept by Him and His grace, to be doing His will and pleasing Him—this cannot possibly be an irregular practice if we are truly devoted to Him.

The clearer the objective of our goal, the better we will be able to accomplish it. Consider the morning watch now as the means to this great end: I want to secure the presence of Christ all the day, to do nothing that can interfere with it. Our success during the day will depend upon the time we spend alone with Him in the morning.

Do not be disturbed if at first this goal appears too difficult and occupies too much of your time. The time you give to bring your daily concerns to the Lord will be richly rewarded. You will return to prayer and scripture reading with new purpose and new faith.

Prayer's Wholehearted Determination

Daniel. . .*prayed* three times a day,
just as he had always done.

Daniel 6:10

As we seek to have unbroken fellowship with God in Christ throughout the day, we will realize that only a definite meeting time with Christ will secure His presence for the day. The essential thing to having a daily quiet time is wholehearted determination, whatever effort or self-denial it may cost. In academic study or athletics, every student needs determined purpose to succeed. Christianity requires, and indeed deserves, not less but more intense devotion. If anything, surely the love of Christ needs the whole heart.

When we make this decision to secure Christ's presence, we will overcome every temptation to be superficial in the keeping of our pledges. Our determination will make the morning watch itself a mighty force in strengthening our character and giving us boldness to resist self-indulgence. It will enable us to enter the inner chamber and shut the door for our communion with Christ. From the morning watch on, this firm resolution will become the keynote of our daily life.

Often we hear the statement that great things are possible to those who know what they want and will it with all their heart. If we have made personal devotion to Christ our goal, we will find the morning hour the place where daily insight into our holy calling is renewed. During this quiet time, we are fortified to walk worthy of His calling. Faith is rewarded by the presence of Christ who is waiting to meet us and take charge of us for the day.

Prayer's Unbroken Fellowship

When Moses came down the mountain. . .
he wasn't aware that his face glowed because
he had spoken to the *Lord* face to face.

EXODUS 34:29

Close and continued prayer fellowship with God will in due time leave its mark and be evident to those around us. Just as Moses did not know that his face shone, we ourselves will be unaware of the light of God shining from us. The sense of God's presence in us may often cause others to feel ill at ease in our company. However, true believers will prove by humility and love that they are indeed persons like those around them. And yet there will be the proof that they are people of God who live in an unseen world.

The blessings of communion with God can easily be lost by entering too deeply into communion with people. The spirit of inner prayer must be carried over into a holy watchfulness throughout the day. We do not know at what hour the enemy will come. This continuance of the morning watch can be maintained by quiet self-restraint, by not giving the reins of our lives over to our natural impulses.

When the abiding sense of God's presence has become the aim of the morning hour, then with deep humility and in loving conversation with those around us, we will pass on into the day's duties with the continuity of unbroken fellowship. It is a great thing to enter the inner chamber, shut the door, and meet the Father in secret. It is a greater thing to open the door again and go out to enjoy God's presence—which nothing can disturb.

PRAYER AND GOD'S WORD

This is what the *LORD* says: ". . .I will bless
those who have humble and contrite hearts,
who tremble at *my* word."

ISAIAH 66:4-2

Many of us are so occupied with how much or how little we
have to say in our prayers that the voice of One speaking is never
heard because it is not expected or waited for. We need to get
into the right frame of mind and have a listening attitude.

In regard to the connection between prayer and the Word
of God in our private devotion, this expression has often been
quoted: "I pray, I speak to God; I read the Bible, God speaks to
me." We need to ask how our scripture reading and praying can
become true fellowship with God.

A prayerful spirit is the spirit to which God will speak. Prayer
prepares the heart for receiving the Word from God Himself, for
the teaching of the Spirit to give the spiritual understanding of
it, for the faith that is made part of its mighty working.

In God's Word we read what God will do in me, how God
would have me come to Him in prayer, assurance that I will be
heard, and what God will do in the world. A prayerful spirit will
be a listening spirit waiting to hear what God says. In true communion with God, His presence and the part He takes must be
as real as my own.

Let us prepare ourselves to pray with a heart that humbly
waits to hear God speak. The greatest blessing in prayer will be
our ceasing to pray to let God speak.

ACCORDING TO GOD'S WILL

And we can be confident that *he* will
listen to us whenever we ask *him* for
anything in line with *his* will.

1 JOHN 5:14

How can we know if we are praying according to God's will? That is an intensely practical question to ask as we take time to pray.

To properly understand 1 John 5:14, we must connect the words "in line with his will" with "ask"—not merely with "anything." Similarly connect "he will listen" with "whenever we ask." Not only the thing asked for but also the disposition and character of the one asking must be in line with God's will. Both the thing asked for and the spirit of asking must be in harmony with God's will.

Jesus' teaching continually connected the answer to prayer with a life that was being lived according to God's will: trusting, forgiving, merciful, humble, believing, asking in His name, abiding in His love, observing/keeping His commands, and having His words abiding within. He also said that if they loved Him and kept His commands, then He would pray to the Father for them. Prayer has power according to the life! A life in line with God's will can ask according to God's will.

When you live according to God's will, you are spiritually able to discern what to ask for. A life yielded to and molded by the will of God will know what and how to pray. Boldness in prayer comes from the assurance that the spirit of asking and the thing asked are both according to the will of God.

COUNTING ON PRAYERS

He will rescue us because you are helping by
praying for us. . . . Many will give thanks to
God because so many people's prayers for
our safety have been answered.

2 CORINTHIANS 1:11

Paul lived in prayer for the churches and had taught them to pray for him and his work, so he felt assured that all would work out well through their prayer and the consequent enablement of the Spirit of Jesus Christ.

He had such a vision of the spiritual unity of the body of Christ through all its members that he felt himself actually dependent upon the prayer of the churches. Where he stood alone he knew God as a God of prayer and had power with Him. But where he had believers to whom he was linked, he felt their prayer to be indispensable for his experience of God's power. It is only when this sense of unity binds minister and people— binds all believers together—that the full power of the Holy Spirit can be expected to work.

We have a lesson here that, if the missionary would train converts in the art of fervent prayer, that missionary would have in them a mighty power to wield against the forces of darkness. On God Paul set his hope that He would continue to deliver him, as they helped him by their prayers.

May we be bound together in the bonds of Jesus Christ in faithfulness to this kind of praying.

INTERCESSION

Pray for each other.

JAMES 5:16

There is a mystery of glory in prayer. On the one hand we see God in His holiness, love, and power—waiting, longing to bless us. On the other hand is a sinful, unworthy human being—asking God in prayer for the very life and love of heaven to dwell in our hearts.

Intercession gives us a lot of joy when we are bold enough to ask God for what we desire for others. Through intercession we seek to bring to others the power of eternal life. This is one of the holiest exercises as God's children, the highest privilege connected with knowing God—the power of being used by God as instruments for His great work.

The Church should seek above everything to cultivate the power of an unceasing prayerfulness on behalf of those without Christ. There is strength in the unity of believers. God will certainly avenge His own who cry day and night to Him. It is when Christians cease looking for help apart from God and aim at being bound together to the throne of God, that the Church will put on her strength to overcome the world. This comes by continuously asking for the power of God's Spirit.

INTERCESSION IN THE PLAN OF REDEMPTION

For *you answer* our prayers,
and to *you* all people will come.

PSALM 65:2

When God gave the world into the power of man, it was His plan that Adam should do nothing except with and through God. God Himself would do all His work in the world through Adam. Adam was to be the owner, master, and ruler of the earth. When sin entered the world Adam's power proved to be a terrible reality. Through him the earth, with the whole race of man, was brought under the curse of sin.

When God made the plan of redemption, His object was to restore man to the place from which he had fallen. God determined that His servants, through the power of intercession, could ask and it would be given them. When Christ became man it was so He might intercede for man. When He left the world, He gave this right of intercession to His children (John 15:16), that whatever they would ask He would do for them. God's intense longing to bless seems to be graciously limited by His dependence on the intercession that rises from the earth.

Christians need to realize they have the right to expect that God will hear prayer. God waits for each individual believer to take his part in the power of intercession to fulfill the petition: "Here on earth, just as it is in heaven." (Matthew 6:10).

GOD SEEKS INTERCESSORS

He was amazed to see that no one
intervened to help the oppressed.

ISAIAH 59:16

God had among His people intercessors to whom He listened. In Isaiah we read of a time of trouble when He sought for an intercessor in vain. There was none who loved the people enough or who had sufficient faith to intercede. If there had been an intercessor, He would have given deliverance; without an intercessor His judgments came down (see Isaiah 64:7; Ezekiel 22:30–31).

The place the intercessor holds in the kingdom of God is of infinite importance. God gives us such power, and yet there are so few who know what it is to take hold of His strength and pray for His blessing.

When Christ had taken His place on the throne, the work of His kingdom was given into the hands of men. Prayer is the highest exercise of Christ's royal prerogative as Priest-King upon the throne. All that He was to do in heaven was to be in fellowship with His people on earth. God waits for His people's intercession.

God rules the world and His Church through the prayers of His people. That God should have made the extension of His kingdom to such a large extent dependent on the faithfulness of His people in prayer is a stupendous mystery and yet an absolute certainty. God calls for intercessors; in His grace He has made His work dependent on them.

CHRIST AS INTERCESSOR

He is able, once and forever, to save everyone
who comes to God through him. He lives
forever to plead with God on their behalf.

HEBREWS 7:25

In His life on earth Christ began His work as intercessor. Think of the high priestly prayer on behalf of His disciples and of all who would believe in His name through them. Think of His words to Peter, "I have pleaded in prayer for you, Simon, that your faith should not fail" (Luke 22:32)—a proof of how intensely personal His intercession is. And on the cross He spoke as intercessor: "Father, forgive these people" (Luke 23:34).

Now that He is seated at God's right hand, He continues, as our great High Priest, the work of intercession without ceasing. Yet He gives His people power to take part in it. Seven times in His farewell discourse He repeated the assurance that He would do what they asked.

The power of heaven was to be at the disciples' disposal. God waited for the disciples to ask for His grace and power. Through the leading of the Holy Spirit they would know what the will of God was. They would learn in faith to pray in His name. He would present their requests to the Father, and through united intercession the Church would be clothed with the power of the Spirit.

THE INTERCESSOR GOD SEEKS

O Jerusalem, I have posted watchmen on your walls;
they will pray to the LORD day and night for the fulfillment
of his promises.

ISAIAH 62:6

Watchmen were ordinarily placed on the walls of a city to give notice to the rulers of coming danger. God appoints watchmen not only to warn men but also to summon His help. The great mark of the intercessors is that they do not rest until God gives an answer. They count upon the assurance that God will answer their prayer.

"Don't you think God will surely give justice to his chosen people who plead with him day and night?" (Luke 18:7). The Church of Christ, under the influence of the power of the world, is losing its influence over its members. There is little proof of God's presence in the conversion of sinners or in the holiness of His people. There is an utter neglect of Christ's call to extend His kingdom.

What can be done to interest young and old in the study of God's Word or to encourage corporate worship? It is because of a lack of prayer that the working of the Spirit is so weak. Only united fervent prayer can change this. If ever there was a time when God's children should cry day and night to Him, it is now. Offer yourself to God for this wonderful work of intercession. Learn to count it the highest privilege of your life to be a channel through whose prayers God's blessing can be brought down to earth.

Name of Jesus—
Power of Intercession

"You haven't done this before. *Ask*, using *my* name,
and you will receive, and you will have abundant joy."

John 16:24

During Christ's life upon earth the disciples knew little of the power of prayer. In Gethsemane they utterly failed. They had no concept of what it was to ask in the name of Jesus and to receive. The Lord promised them that in the future they would be able to pray with such a power that they may ask what they would, and it would be given.

"You haven't done this before. Ask, using my name, and you will receive." These two conditions are still found in the Church. We lack knowledge of our oneness with Christ and of the Holy Spirit as the Spirit of prayer so that we make no attempt to claim the promises Christ gives. But when God's children know what it is to abide in Christ and to yield to the Holy Spirit, we begin to learn that God will give His power in answer to prayer.

Faith in the power of Jesus' name and our right to use it gives us courage to be intercessors.

Intense and unceasing prayerfulness is the essential mark of the healthy spiritual life. The power of all-prevailing intercession will indeed be the portion of those who live only for their Lord.

GOD'S WILL AND OURS

"Your will be done."

MATTHEW 26:42

When God created man with the power to will and choose what he should be, He limited Himself in the exercise of His will. And when man had fallen and yielded himself to the will of God's enemy, God in His love set about the great work of winning man back. As in God, so in man, desire is the great moving power. Just as man had yielded himself to a life of desire after the things of the earth and the flesh, God desired to redeem him and to educate him into a life of harmony with Himself.

When Christ came into this world, He reproduced the divine desires in His human nature. He yielded Himself up to the perfect fulfillment of all that God wanted. When He prayed "Your will be done," He surrendered to being forsaken by God so that Satan might be conquered and deliverance obtained. It was in complete harmony between the Father and the Son when the Son said, "Your will of love be done" and redemption was accomplished.

As believers we appropriate that great work of redemption when we pray, "Your will be done in heaven as on earth."

THE BLESSEDNESS OF A
LIFE OF INTERCESSION

Take no rest, all you who pray. Give the
Lord no rest until *he* makes Jerusalem the
object of praise throughout the earth.

ISAIAH 62:6-7

What a gift of grace to be allowed to work with God in intercession for the needs of others! What a blessing to mingle my prayers with His! What an honor to have power with God in heaven for those who do not know Christ. What a privilege to bring to Him the Church, individuals, ministers, or missionaries, and plead on their behalf until He entrusts me with the answer!

As God's children we are blessed to pray together until victory is gained over difficulties here on earth or over the powers of darkness!

For a long time we may have thought of prayer simply as a means of supplying our needs in life. May God help us to see the place intercession takes in His divine counsel and in His work for the kingdom. May our hearts really feel that there is no honor or joy on earth at all equal to the unspeakable privilege of waiting upon God and interceding for the blessing He delights to give!

Paul as an Intercessor

I *fall* to my knees and *pray* to the Father. . .that from *his*
glorious, unlimited resources *he* will give you mighty inner
strength through *his Holy Spirit.*

Ephesians 3:14, 16

We think of Paul as the great missionary, writer, apostle. We usually do not think of him as the intercessor who, through prayer, obtained the power that rested on all his activities.

We see above what he wrote to the Ephesians. He told the Thessalonians (1 Thessalonians 3:10): "Night and day we pray earnestly for you, asking God to let us see you again to fill up anything that may still be missing in your faith." To the Romans (1:9): "Day and night I bring you and your needs in prayer to God." To the Philippians (1:4): "I always pray for you." And to the Colossians (1:9): "So we have continued praying for you."

Paul believed in the power of his intercession for others. He also believed in the blessing that others would bring him. "I urge you in the name of our Lord Jesus Christ to join me in my struggle by praying to God for me" (Romans 15:30). "For I know that as you pray for me and as the Spirit of Jesus Christ helps me, this will all turn out for my deliverance" (Philippians 1:19).

The whole relationship between pastor and people depends on united, continual prayerfulness. When ministers and people become conscious of the power and blessing of the Holy Spirit that comes from their prayer, then the church will begin to know what pentecostal, apostolic Christianity is.

INTERCESSION FOR
INDIVIDUAL SOULS

Yet the time will come when the *Lord* will gather them together
one by one like handpicked grain.

ISAIAH 27:12

Many individual believers do not understand that it is necessary
for them to testify to others in order to strengthen their own
spiritual lives as well as to bring others to Christ. Intercession
for those around us, and for the church and its mission, needs
restoration to its right place in the Christian life!

Prayer is indispensable to what God in heaven desires to do
on earth. Intercession is the main element in the conversion of
souls. All our efforts are in vain without the power of the Holy
Spirit given in answer to prayer. When ministers and people
unite in a covenant of prayer and testimony, the Church will
flourish.

What can we do to stir up the spirit of intercession? Begin
to get an insight into the need and the power of intercession.
Intercede on behalf of single individuals. Pray for your children,
your relatives, friends, and for all with whom you come into
contact. If you feel you don't have power to intercede, ask the
Holy Spirit for that power. God wants every redeemed child of
His to intercede for those who do not know Him.

Pray fervently that God will give you the power of His Holy
Spirit for this ministry of intercession.

MISSIONARY INTERCESSION

So after more fasting and prayer, the men *laid* their hands on
them and *sent* them on their way.

ACTS 13:3

How do we multiply the number of Christians who will intercede for those without Christ?—that is the supreme question
of foreign missions. Those who love this work will pray unceasingly for its triumph.

Missions has its root in the love of Christ. God's children
should be wholehearted in seeking to bring Christ's love to all
mankind. Intercession is the chief means appointed by God to
bring the great redemption within the reach of all.

Pray for the missionaries that their witness may be clear and
strong. Pray that they may be men and women of prayer, filled with
love, in whom the power of the spiritual life is made manifest.

Pray for national Christians that they may know the glory
of the mystery among unbelievers—"Christ lives in you, and
this is your assurance that you will share in his glory" (Colossians 1:27). Pray for students in the schools, that the teaching
of God's Word may be in power. Pray especially for the national
pastors and evangelists that the Holy Spirit may fill them to be
witnesses for Christ in their country.

Pray, above all, for the Church of Christ that it may be lifted
out of its indifference. Pray that every believer may understand
that the one object of life is to help make Christ King on the
earth.

THE GRACE OF INTERCESSION

Devote yourselves to prayer with an alert mind and a thankful heart. Don't forget to pray for us, too.

COLOSSIANS 4:2–3

There is nothing that can bring us nearer to God and lead us deeper into His love than the work of intercession. Nothing gives us a higher experience of God than pouring out our hearts to Him in prayer for men and women. Nothing can so closely connect us to Jesus Christ and give us the experience of His power and Spirit as yielding our lives to the work of bringing redemption into the lives of others. There is nothing in which we will know more of the working of the Holy Spirit than the prayer breathed by Him into our hearts, "Abba, Father."

As we become a living sacrifice before God with the persistent prayer for His abundant blessing, God will be glorified. In intercession, our souls will reach their highest destiny and God's kingdom will come.

As God's children daily pray together that God will make His Church a light to those who are sitting in darkness, we will experience unity and power in the Body of Christ. How little we realize what we are losing in not living in fervent intercession!

Christ lives in heaven to pray—asking the fullness of the Spirit for His people. God delights in nothing as much as in prayer. Believe that the highest blessings of heaven will be given to us as we pray more.

UNCEASING INTERCESSION

Keep on praying.

1 THESSALONIANS 5:17

The average Christian has a very different standard regarding a life of service to God than that which scripture gives us. We think about our personal safety—grace to pardon our sin and to secure our entrance into heaven. The Bible's standard is that we surrender ourselves, our time, our thoughts, and our love to God.

To the average Christian the command "keep on praying" is a needless and impossible life of perfection. Who can do it? We can get to heaven without it.

However, to the true believer that command holds the promise of the highest happiness and of a life crowned by all the blessings that come through intercession. Through perseverance it becomes the highest aim and joy upon earth.

"Keep on praying." Take that word in faith as a promise of what God's Spirit will work in us. Let it become our heavenly calling. Christ said, "I in them and you in me." Let us believe that just as the Father worked in Him, Christ will work and pray in us. As the faith of our calling fills our hearts we literally will begin to feel there is nothing on earth to be compared with the privilege of walking without interruption in His holy presence, bringing others around us to the footstool of His throne and receiving His power.

THE FULFILLMENT
OF GOD'S DESIRES

For the *Lord* has chosen Jerusalem;
he has desired it as *his* home.

PSALM 132:13

The one great desire of God that moved Him in the work of redemption was that His heart longed for us to dwell with Him and in Him. He said to Moses: "I want the people of Israel to build me a sacred residence where I can live among them" (Exodus 25:8). As His children we are called to yield ourselves to God to dwell in us and to bring others to become His habitation.

What an honor to find our lives and our joy in bringing others to Christ in whom God may find His heart's delight: "I will live here, for this is the place I desired."

This is what we can do. We can ask God to give those around us His Holy Spirit. It is God's great plan that we will build Him a habitation. God will give His power and blessing in answer to the unceasing intercession of His children. As this desire of God fills us, we will give ourselves totally to work for its fulfillment.

Let us begin, as never before, to pray for our children, for those around us, and for all the world. Pray not only because we love them but also because God longs for them. He gives us the honor of being the channels through whom His blessing is brought down.

MY GREAT DESIRE

The thing I *seek* most—is to live in the
house of the *LORD* all the days of my
life. . . .meditating in *his* Temple.

PSALM 27:4

Psalm 27:4 is our response to God's desire to dwell in us. When the desire of God begins to rule our life, our desire is to live in the house of the Lord all the days of our life, to delight in the Lord's perfections, to meditate in His temple, and to learn what God means when He speaks.

The more we realize that God's desire is to give His rest, and the more our desire is to dwell in His temple and behold His beauty, the more the Spirit of prayer will be ours. Whether we think of our church and country, of our home and school, of the saved and their needs, or the unsaved and their danger, the thought that God is longing to find His home and His rest in the hearts of men will urge us to pray.

All the thoughts of our weakness and unworthiness will be swallowed up in the wonderful assurance that He has said of human hearts: "This is my home where I will live forever. . .I will live here, for this is the place I desired" (Psalm 132:14).

God has made fervent, persistent prayer indispensable to His purpose being fulfilled. Thank God for this divine partnership in which God commits the fulfillment of His desires to our keeping.

Intercession Day and Night

"Don't you think *God* will surely give justice to *his* chosen
people who plead with *him* day and night?
Will *he* keep putting them off?"

Luke 18:7

When Nehemiah heard of the destruction of Jerusalem, he cried
to God, "Listen to my prayer! Look down and see me praying night and day for your people Israel" (Nehemiah 1:6). God
said of the watchmen on the walls of Jerusalem: "They will pray
to the Lord day and night for the fulfillment of his promises"
(Isaiah 62:6). Paul writes: "Night and day we pray earnestly for
you. . .[that] Christ will make your hearts strong, blameless, and
holy" (1 Thessalonians 3:10, 13).

Is such prayer, night and day, really needed and really possible? Most assuredly it is, when our life has been so blessed that
nothing can keep us from sacrificing all to intercede.

When we as children of God begin to get a real vision into
the need of the church and of the world, a vision of the outpouring of God's love, a vision of the power of true intercession, a
vision of the honor of being allowed to take part in that work, it
comes as a matter of course that we regard this work as the most
divine thing upon earth.

There is nothing more worth living for than this—how to
satisfy God in His longing for human fellowship and love, and
how to win hearts to be His dwelling place. Let's not rest until
we have found a place for the Mighty One in our hearts and
have yielded ourselves to the work of intercession!

A Call for Decision

"Ask me and I will tell you some remarkable secrets about what is going to happen here."

JEREMIAH 33:3

Are you willing to give yourself totally to the power of Jesus Christ to make intercession for God's Church and for a dying world? Will you make this the main object of your life? Is it too much to yield your life to the Lord who gave Himself for you?

Intercession should not take a subordinate place in the teaching and practice of the Church with its ministers and members. It is of such supreme importance as to make it an essential, altogether indispensable element in the true Christian life. There can be no doubt about this to those who take God's Word in its full meaning.

Child of God, God counts upon you to take your place before His throne as an intercessor. Renew the consciousness of your holy calling as a royal priesthood. Begin to live life in the assurance that intercession is the highest privilege a man or woman can desire. Accept the Word with great expectation: "Ask me and I will tell you some remarkable secrets about what is going to happen here."

GOD WILL HEAR ME

But the *LORD* still *waits* for you to come to *him*
so *he* can show you *his* love and compassion. . . .
He will be gracious if you ask for help. *He* will respond
instantly to the sound of your cries.

ISAIAH 30:18–19

The power of prayer rests in the faith that God hears prayer. In more than one sense this is true. This faith gives us courage to pray. This faith gives us power to prevail with God. The moment I am assured that God hears me, too, I feel drawn to pray and to persevere in prayer. I feel strong to claim and to take in faith the answer God gives.

One reason for the lack of prayer is the want of the living, joyous assurance, "God will hear me." If only God's servants would get a vision of the living God waiting to grant their request. If they could see that He longs to bestow all the heavenly gifts of the Spirit they are in need of. Then they would set aside everything and make time and room for this power that can ensure heavenly blessing—the prayer of faith!

When you say in faith "God will hear me!" nothing can keep you from prayer. You know that what you cannot do on earth can and will be done for you from heaven. Let each one of us bow in stillness before God and wait on Him to reveal Himself as the prayer-hearing God. In His presence the wondrous thoughts gathering round the central truth will unfold themselves to us.

A WONDERFUL CERTAINTY

As for me, I *look* to the LORD for help.
I *wait* confidently for God to save me.

MICAH 7:7

God will hear me. What a wonderful certainty! We have God's Word for it. We have thousands of witnesses that have found it true. We have experienced it ourselves. The Son of God came from heaven with the message that if we ask, the Father will give. Christ prayed on earth; now He is in heaven interceding for us. God hears prayer—God delights in hearing our prayer. He has allowed His people to be tried so that they are compelled to cry to Him and learn to know Him as the hearer of prayer.

We should confess with shame how little we have believed this truth. We have failed to receive it into our hearts. Accepting a truth is not enough; the living God must be revealed by it so that our whole life is spent in His presence. We must live with an awareness as clear as in a little child toward its earthly parent—I know for certain my Father hears me.

By experience you know how little an intellectual understanding of truth has profited you. Ask God to reveal Himself to you. If you want to live a different prayer life, bow to worship God in silence each time before you pray. Wait there until you have a deep consciousness of His nearness and His readiness to answer. After that you can begin to pray with the words, "God will hear me!"

A WONDROUS GRACE

The *LORD* will answer when I *call* to *him*.

PSALM 4:3

God will hear me. What a wondrous grace! Think of God in His infinite majesty, His altogether incomprehensible glory, His unapproachable holiness, sitting on a throne of grace, waiting to be gracious, inviting and encouraging you to pray with His promise: "Ask me and I will tell you some remarkable secrets about what is going to happen here" (Jeremiah 33:3).

Think of yourself in your transgressions as a sinner and in your unworthiness as a saint. Praise God for the grace which allows you to say boldly of your prayer for yourself and others, "God will hear me."

Think of what you can accomplish in this wonderful intimacy with God. God has united you with Christ. In Him you have your confidence. On the throne He prays with you and for you. You pray with Him and in Him. His worth and the Father's delight in hearing Him are the measure of your confidence, your assurance of being heard.

There is more. When you don't know what to pray the Holy Spirit is sent into your heart to cry, "Abba, Father," and to be in you a Spirit of prayer. In all your unworthiness, you are as acceptable as Christ Himself. In your ignorance and weakness, the Spirit is making intercession according to God within you.

A Deep Mystery

I am *praying* to *you* because
I *know you* will answer, O *God*.

God will hear me. What a deep mystery! There are difficulties that arise and perplex the heart. There is the question of God's sovereign will. How can our wishes change His perfect will? He knows what is best and loves to give us the very best. How can our prayer change what He has ordained?

What is the need of persevering in prayer? If God is infinite love, delighting to give, why is there need for pleading, for urgency and long delay in answering our prayers?

What of the multitude of apparently unanswered prayers? Many have pleaded for loved ones and they die unsaved. Many cry for physical healing without result. This tries our faith and makes us hesitate when we say, "God will hear me."

Prayer is a deep spiritual mystery. Answers can be given that remove some of the difficulty from our questions but, as little as we can comprehend of God, we can comprehend one of the most wonderful of His attributes—He hears prayer. It is a spiritual mystery.

God hears because we pray in His Son and because the Holy Spirit prays in us. If we have believed in Christ and the Holy Spirit, we should not hesitate to believe in the power of our prayer, too. We can believe and rejoice in it, even where every question is not yet answered. We need to surrender our questions to God's love, trust His faithfulness, and obey His command to pray without ceasing.

A BLESSED PROSPECT

I fall to my knees and pray to the Father. . .that from his glorious, unlimited resources he will give you mighty inner strength through his Holy Spirit.

EPHESIANS 3:14–16

God will hear me—what a blessed prospect! The failures of my past life have been due to lack of this faith. Especially in the work of intercession, I did not live in the full faith of the assurance that "God will hear me!" I begin to see it and believe it. All can be different.

Commonplace and insignificant though I am, I have access to this infinite God with the confidence that He hears me. I will pray for others for I am sure my God will listen to me; my God will hear me.

What a prospect before me—every anxiety exchanged for the peace of God. We can know that even when the answer is long delayed and there is a call for patient, persevering prayer, the truth remains infallibly sure—God will hear me.

If only we could all give prayer its place, give faith in God its place, or, rather, give the prayer-hearing God His place! This is the one great thing that those who begin to awaken to the urgent need for prayer ought to pray for.

When God first poured out the Spirit on His praying people, He formulated the law for all time: In the degree that you pray you will receive the Spirit.

Great Worship

Worship God!

Revelation 22:9

Why is it that prayer and intercession with God are not a greater joy and delight? One answer to this question undoubtedly is: We know God too little. In our prayer, His presence is not the chief thing our heart is seeking. And yet it should be. Often when we pray, we think mostly of ourselves, our needs, our desires. But we forget that in every prayer, God must be first, must be all.

So how is one to attain this nearness to God and fellowship with Him? The answer is simple: We must give God time to make Himself known to us. Believe with your whole heart, that just as you present yourself to God as a supplicant, so God presents Himself to you as the hearer of prayer. But you cannot realize this unless you give Him time and quiet.

It is not in the multitude or the earnestness of your words in which prayer has its power. Your prayer has its power in the living faith that God Himself is taking you and your prayer into His loving heart. He Himself will give the assurance that in His time your prayer will be heard.

Begin your day with these words: "To you, O LORD, I lift up my soul" (Psalm 25:1). "I thirst for God, the living God" (Psalm 42:2).

INTERCESSION AND ADORATION

Worship the LORD in all his holy splendor.

PSALM 96:9

The better we know God, the more wonderful our insight into the power of intercession becomes. We begin to understand that it is the greatest means by which man can take part in carrying out God's purpose. God has entrusted the whole of His redemption in Christ to His people to make known and to communicate to men. In all this, intercession is the chief and essential element. Through it, His servants receive the power of the Spirit as their power for service.

The clearer the insight into this great purpose of God, the more we will sense the need to enter into God's presence in the spirit of humble worship and holy adoration. The more we take time to abide in God's presence—to enter fully into His mind and will, to get our whole soul possessed by the thought of His glorious purpose—the stronger our faith will become that God Himself will work out all the good pleasure of His will through our prayers.

Thus, the secret of true adoration can only be known by the soul that gives time to tarry in God's presence and that yields itself to God for Him to reveal Himself. Adoration will indeed fit us for the great work of making God's glory known.

SILENT ADORATION

I *wait* quietly before *God*. . . . I *wait* quietly
before *God*, for my hope is in *him*.

PSALM 62:4, 5

When we in our littleness and God in His glory meet, we all understand that what God says has infinitely more worth than what a person says. And yet our prayer so often consists of what we need that we give God no time to speak to us.

It is a great lesson to learn that to be silent before God is the secret of true adoration. It is only as the soul bows itself before Him in honor and reverence that the heart will be opened to receive the divine impression of the nearness of God and of the working of His power.

Such worship of God is the surest way to give Him the glory that is due Him. It will lead to a blessedness that can only be found in quiet prayer. Do not think that it is time lost. Do not abandon it if at first it appears difficult or fruitless. Be assured that it brings you into the right relationship with God. It opens the way to fellowship with Him. It leads to the blessed assurance that He is looking on you in tender love and working in you with a divine power.

As you become more accustomed to it, you will experience His presence abiding with you all day long, and people will begin to sense that you have been with God.

ALONE WITH GOD

He went higher into the hills alone.

Human beings need to be alone with God. Our fall consisted in our being brought, through the lust of the flesh and the world, under the power of things visible and temporal. Our restoration through salvation is meant to bring us back to the Father's love and fellowship.

We need to be alone with God, to yield ourselves to the presence and the power of His holiness. Christ on earth needed it. He could not live the life of a Son here in the flesh without at times separating Himself entirely from His surroundings and being alone with God. How much more must this be indispensable to us!

Alone with God—that is the secret of true power in prayer. There is no true holiness, no clothing with the Holy Spirit and with power, without being alone daily with God.

When our Lord Jesus gave us the command to pray to our Father in secret, He gave us the promise that the Father would hear such prayers and mightily answer them in our life before others. What a privilege it is to begin every morning with intimate prayer. Let it be the one thing our hearts are set on—seeing, finding, and meeting God alone. The time will come when you will be amazed at the thought that one could suggest five minutes was enough.

THE KNOWLEDGE OF GOD

"This is the way to have eternal life—to know *you*,
the only true *God*, and *Jesus Christ*,
the one *you sent* to earth."

JOHN 17:3

The knowledge of God is absolutely necessary for the spiritual life. It is life eternal. Not the intellectual knowledge we receive from others or through our own power of thought, but the living, experiential knowledge in which God makes Himself known to the soul.

Why is it that we so seldom experience this life-giving power of the true knowledge of God? Because we do not give God time enough to reveal Himself to us. When we pray, we think we know exactly how to speak to God. Yet we forget that one of the very first things in prayer is to be silent before God. It is then that He will reveal Himself. To know God in the personal experience of His presence and love is life indeed.

Just as the sun rising each morning is the pledge of light throughout the day, so the quiet time of waiting upon God will be the pledge of His presence and His power resting on us all day.

Learn this great lesson that the sun proclaims each day: As the sun on a cold day shines on us and imparts its warmth, believe that the living God will work in you with His love and His almighty power. God will reveal Himself as life and light and joy and strength to the soul that waits upon Him.

GOD THE FATHER

"Baptizing them in the name of the
Father and the *Son* and the *Holy Spirit."*

MATTHEW 28:19

It is important to realize that the doctrine of the Holy Trinity has a deep devotional aspect. As we think of God, we remember the inconceivable distance that separates Him in His holiness from sinful humans, and we bow in deep contrition and holy fear. As we think of Christ the Son, we remember the inconceivable nearness in which He came to be born of a woman and to die the accursed death and so to be inseparably joined to us for all eternity. And as we think of the Holy Spirit, we remember the inconceivable blessedness of God dwelling in us and making us His home and His temple throughout eternity.

When Christ taught us to say "Our Father in heaven," He immediately added, "may your name be honored" (Matthew 6:9). As God is holy, so also are we to be holy. And there is no way of becoming holy without considering that name to be most holy and drawing near to Him in prayer.

How often we speak that name without any sense of the unspeakable privilege of our relationship to God. If we would just take time to come into contact with God and to worship Him in His Fatherly love, that intimate place of communion would become to us the gate of heaven.

GOD THE SON

May grace and peace be yours from
God our *Father* and the *Lord Jesus Christ*.

ROMANS 1:7

It is remarkable that the Apostle Paul in each of his thirteen Epistles writes: "May grace and peace be yours from God our Father and the Lord Jesus Christ." He had such a deep sense of the inseparable oneness of the Father and the Son in the work of grace that in each opening benediction he refers to both.

This is a lesson of the utmost importance. There may be times in the Christian life when one thinks chiefly of God the Father and prays to Him. But later on we realize that it may cause spiritual loss if we do not grasp this truth: It is only through faith in Christ and in living with Him that we can enjoy a full and abiding fellowship with God.

If you desire to know and worship God, seek Him and worship Him in Christ. And if you seek Christ, seek Him and worship Him in God. Then you will understand what it is to have "your life hidden with Christ in God." You will also discover that the fellowship and adoration of Christ is indispensable to the full knowledge of the love and holiness of God.

Take time to meditate, to pray, to expect all from God the Father who sits upon the throne and from the Lord Jesus Christ, the Lamb in the midst of the throne. Then you will learn to truly worship God.

GOD THE HOLY SPIRIT

Now all of us. . .may come to the *Father*
through the same *Holy Spirit* because
of what *Christ* has done for us.

EPHESIANS 2:18

In our communion with God, we must guard against the danger of seeking to know God and Christ in the power of our intellect or emotions. The Holy Spirit has been given for the express purpose that we "may come to the Father through the same Holy Spirit because of what Christ has done for us." We will find that our prayer is in vain if we do not wait for the guidance of the Spirit.

Remember that one of the Holy Spirit's objectives is to teach us to pray. He makes fellowship with the Father and the Son a wonderful reality. As you pray, give yourself wholly to His guidance as your Teacher in all your intercession and adoration.

When Christ said, "Receive the Holy Spirit" (John 20:22), it was, in part, to strengthen and prepare the disciples for the ten days of prayer and for their receiving the fullness of the Spirit. This suggests three things we ought to remember when we draw near to God in prayer:

First—pray in the confidence that the Holy Spirit lives in us, and yield ourselves to His leading.

Second—believe that the "greater works" of the Spirit for the enlightening and strengthening of the spiritual life will be given in answer to prayer.

Third—believe that through the Spirit, in unity with all God's children, we may ask and expect the mighty workings of that Spirit on His Church and people.

HALF AN HOUR SILENCE IN HEAVEN

There was silence throughout heaven for about
half an hour. Then. . .incense was given to him
to mix with the prayers of God's people.

REVELATION 8:1, 3

There was silence in heaven for about half an hour—to bring the prayers of the saints before God. Many of God's children have also felt the absolute need of silence and withdrawal from the things of earth for half an hour—to present their prayers before God. In so doing, they have been strengthened for their daily work.

How often the complaint is heard that there is no time for prayer. Yet often the confession is made that, even if time could be found, one feels unable to spend the time in real communion with God. Don't think, "I will not know how to spend the time." Just believe that, if you bow in silence before God, He will reveal Himself to you.

If you need help, read some passages of scripture and let God's Word speak to you. Then bow in deepest humility before God and wait on Him. He will begin to work within you as you intercede for those whom He has laid on your heart. Keep praying, though the time may seem long. God will surely meet you.

Is it not worth the trouble to take half an hour alone with God? In heaven itself there was need for half an hour's silence to present the prayers of the saints before God. If you persevere, you may find the half hour that seems the most difficult may become the most blessed in your whole life.

GOD IS GREAT

For *you* are great and *perform* great miracles.
You alone are *God*.

PSALM 86:10

Men and women of science, in studying nature, require years of labor to grasp the magnitude of the universe. Isn't God more glorious and worthy? And shouldn't we take the time to know and adore His greatness?

Our knowledge of God's greatness is so superficial. We do not allow ourselves time to bow before Him. Therefore we do not come under the deep impression of His incomprehensible majesty and glory.

Meditate on the following text until you are filled with some sense of what a glorious being God is: "Great is the LORD! He is most worthy of praise! His greatness is beyond discovery!" (Psalm 145:3).

Take time for the meaning of these words to master your heart. Then bow in speechless adoration before God and say, "O Sovereign LORD! . . . Nothing is too hard for you! . . . You are the great and powerful God, the LORD Almighty. You have all wisdom and do great and mighty miracles" (Jeremiah 32:17–19). And hear God's answer: "I am the LORD, the God of all the peoples of the world. Is anything too hard for me?" (v. 27).

The true comprehension of God's greatness will take time. But if our faith grows strong in the knowledge of what a great and powerful God we have, we will be compelled to worship before this great and mighty God.

THE FEAR OF GOD

Happy are those who fear the *Lord*. Yes, happy are those who delight in doing what *he* commands.

PSALM 112:1

The fear of God—these words characterize the religion of the Old Testament and the foundation which it laid for the more abundant life of the New Testament. The gift of holy fear should still be the great desire of the child of God today.

Paul more than once gives fear a high place in the Christian life: "put into action God's saving work in your lives, obeying God with deep reverence and fear" (Philippians 2:12). "Let us work toward complete purity because we fear God" (2 Corinthians 7:1).

It has often been said that the lack of the fear of God is one of the things which most characterizes us today. It is no wonder then that we lack the passion for the reading of God's Word and the worship in His house. We feel the absence of that spirit of continuous prayer which marked the early church. We need texts like the one at the beginning of this reading to impress upon us the need for a deep fear of God, leading to an unceasing prayerfulness.

As we pray, let us earnestly cultivate the fear of God. Then take the words "Happy are those who fear the Lord" into our hearts. Believe that it is one of the essential elements of the life of faith.

THE HOLINESS OF GOD

"Holy *Father, keep* them and *care* for them. . . . Make them pure and holy by teaching them *your* words of truth."

JOHN 17:11, 17

Christ ever lives to pray this great prayer found in the gospel of John. Expect and appropriate God's answer. Hear the words of the Apostle Paul: "Christ will make your hearts strong, blameless, and holy when you stand before God" (1 Thessalonians 3:13). "Now may the God of peace make you holy in every way, and may your whole spirit and soul and body be kept blameless" (1 Thessalonians 5:23).

God's holiness has been revealed in the Old Testament. In the New, we find the holiness of God's people in Christ, through the cleansing of the Spirit. "We are writing to the church of God in Corinth, you who have been called by God to be his own holy people. He made you holy by means of Christ Jesus" (1 Corinthians 1:2).

Oh, that we understood the blessedness of saying: "Be holy because I am holy." For this purpose the triune God has revealed Himself to us, through the Son and the Holy Spirit. Let us use the word "holy" with great reverence of God, and then with holy desire, for ourselves.

Bow before God in holy fear, and then in complete faith, pray this prayer of promise: "The God of peace make you holy in every way. . .God, who calls you, is faithful; he will do this" (1 Thessalonians 5:23–24). What a privilege to speak these words to God. Wait upon Him until, through the working of the Spirit, these words live in your heart. Then you will begin to know something of the holiness of God.

SIN

I was the worst of them all {sinners}. Oh, how kind and gracious the *Lord* was! *He filled* me completely with faith and the love of *Christ Jesus*.

1 TIMOTHY 1:14–15

Never forget for a moment that your whole relationship to God depends on what you think of sin and of yourself as a redeemed sinner. It is sin that makes God's holiness so awful. It is sin that makes God's holiness so glorious, because He has said: "So set yourselves apart to be holy, for I, the LORD, am your God. . . . I am the LORD, who makes you holy" (Leviticus 20:7–8).

It is sin that called forth the wonderful love of God in not sparing His Son.

It was sin that nailed Jesus to the cross and revealed the depth and the power of the love with which He loved.

It is the thought of sin, ever surrounding you and seeking to tempt you, that will give fervency to your prayer and urgency to the faith that hides itself in Christ.

It is the thought of sin that makes Christ so unspeakably precious. It keeps you every moment dependent on His grace and gives you the claim to be more than conqueror through Him that loved us.

It is the thought of sin that calls to us to thank God with the broken and contrite heart, which God will not despise.

As you fellowship with God in prayer, His one aim is to deliver and keep you fully from sin's power and to lift you up into His likeness and His infinite love.

THE LOVE OF GOD

God is love, and all who live in love
live in *God*, and *God lives* in them.

1 JOHN 4:16

The most wonderful word in heaven is love—for God is love. And the most wonderful word in the inner chamber must be love—for the God who meets us there is love.

What is love? It is the deep desire to give itself for the beloved. Love finds its joy in imparting all that it has to make the loved one happy. And the heavenly Father, who offers to meet us in the inner chamber, has no other object than to fill our hearts with His love.

All the other attributes of God find in His love their highest glory. The full blessing of the inner chamber is nothing less than a life in the abundant love of God. Because of this we should approach God with faith in His love. As you set yourself to pray, seek to exercise great and unbounded faith in the love of God.

Take time in silence to meditate on the wonderful revelation of God's love in Christ until you are filled with the spirit of worship and wonder. Take time to believe the precious truth: "He has given us the Holy Spirit to fill our hearts with his love" (Romans 5:5).

As you pray, be assured of this: Your heavenly Father longs to manifest His love to you. Be deeply convinced that He can and will do it.

THE HOLY TRINITY

God the *Father* chose you long ago,
and the *Spirit* has made you holy.
As a result, you have obeyed *Jesus Christ*.

1 PETER 1:2

Here we have one of the texts in which the great truth of the Trinity is seen to lie at the very root of our spiritual life. We have been speaking especially of the adoration of God the Father and the need for sufficient time each day to worship Him in some of His glorious attributes. But we must remind ourselves that, in all our communion with the Father, the presence and the power of the Son and the Spirit are absolutely necessary.

We must understand how our communion with the Father is conditioned by the active and personal presence and working of the Lord Jesus. It takes time to become fully conscious of the need we have of Him in every approach to God. But we can have confidence in the work that He is doing in us and assurance of His intimate love and presence as we make intercession.

So, too, the Holy Spirit, working in the depth of our heart, is the One who is able to reveal the Son within us. Through Him alone we have the power to know what and how to pray. Through Him we have the assurance that our prayer has been accepted.

Dear Christian, it is in tarrying in the secret of God's presence that you receive grace to abide in Christ and to be led by His Spirit. What food for thought—and worship!

The Word of God

For the word of *God* is full of living power.

HEBREWS 4:12

When communing with God, His Word and prayer are both indispensable and should not be separated. In His Word, God speaks to me; in prayer, I speak to God.

The Word teaches me to know the God to whom I pray; it teaches me how He would have me pray. It gives me precious promises to encourage me in prayer. It often gives me wonderful answers to prayer.

The more I pray, the more I feel my need of the Word and rejoice in it. The more I read God's Word, the more I have to pray about and the more power I have in prayer. One great cause of prayerlessness is that we read God's Word too little or only superficially or in the light of human wisdom.

It is the Holy Spirit through whom the Word has been spoken, who is also the Spirit of prayer. He will teach me how to receive the Word and how to approach God.

What power and inspiration would be ours if we only took God's Word as from Himself, turning it into prayer and definitely expecting an answer. It is in the intimacy of God's presence and by the Holy Spirit that God's Word will become our delight and our strength.

Scripture Index